Romeo and Juliet

William Shakespeare

Guide written and developed by
John Mahoney and Stewart Martin

BPP Letts Educational Ltd

First published 1987
Reprinted 1992, 1993
by BPP (Letts Educational) Ltd
Aldine House, Aldine Place
London W12 8AW

Illustration: Peter McClure

Stewart Martin is an Honours graduate of Lancaster University, where he read English
and Sociology. He has worked both in the UK and abroad as a writer, a teacher, and an
educational consultant. He is married with three children, and is currently deputy
headmaster at Ossett School in West Yorkshire.

John Mahoney has taught English for twenty years. He has been head of English
department in three schools and has wide experience of preparing students at all levels
for most examination boards. He has worked both in the UK and North America
producing educational books and computer software on English language and literature.

British Library Cataloguing in Publication Data
Mahoney, John
Romeo and Juliet: William Shakespeare:
guide – (Guides to literature)
I. Shakespeare, William. Romeo and Juliet
I. Title II. Martin, Stewart III. Series
822.3' PR2831

ISBN 1 85758 145 8

Printed and bound in Great Britain by
Staples Printers St Albans Ltd

Contents

To the student

This study companion to your English Literature text acts as a guide to the novel or play being studied. It suggests ways in which you can explore content and context, and focuses your attention on those matters which will lead to an understanding, appreciative and sensitive response to the work of literature being studied.

Whilst covering all those aspects dealt with in the traditional-style study aid, more importantly, it is a flexible companion to study, enabling you to organize the patterns of study and priorities which reflect your particular needs at any given moment.

Whilst in many places descriptive, it is never prescriptive, always encouraging a sensitive personal response to a work of literature, rather than the shallow repetition of others' opinions. Such objectives have always been those of the good teacher, and have always assisted the student to gain high grades in 16+ examinations in English literature. These same factors are also relevant to students who are doing coursework in English literature for the purposes of continual assessment.

The major part of this guide is the 'Commentary' where you will find a detailed commentary and analysis of all the important things you should know and study for your examination. There is also a section giving practical help on how to study a set text, write the type of essay that will gain high marks, prepare coursework and a guide to sitting examinations.

Used sensibly, this guide will be invaluable in your studies and help ensure your success in the course.

With Shakespearian plays there are variations in the text from edition to edition. However, any edition of *Romeo and Juliet* can be used with this guide if you refer to the actual quotation line rather than to the act, scene and line reference.

William Shakespeare

Not much is known for certain about Shakespeare's private life and it matters little for an enjoyment of his plays. We know that he was born in 1564 and brought up in Stratford-on-Avon, that he went to London in 1586, wrote poetry, acted in the theatre and was co-author of some plays. He seems to have started writing plays under his own name in about 1591. He was a prolific writer, and within two or three years he produced several comedies and histories, as well as a sort of horror tragedy. Compared with the work of previous playwrights these early plays were outstanding for their style and characterization, but for Shakespeare they were merely an apprenticeship for his later work. He died in 1616.

His genius seemed to flower in 1595 with the production of *Romeo and Juliet*, his first tragedy approaching the classical type, and a kind of half-way house to the four great tragedies (*Hamlet, Lear, Othello* and *Macbeth*) of his maturity a few years later. Since his day, critics have found fault with the plot of *Romeo and Juliet*, the play's structure, Shakespeare's apparently obsessive punning, his anachronisms, the morality of the play, and even Juliet's age! The fact remains that when it was performed for the first time no play so intense, so poetical, so well-considered in terms of character could ever have been seen before, and that the passion and the pity still come alive for us today, across all the centuries.

The sources of the plot

Shakespeare was not concerned with originality of plot, neither did his audience expect it; Bible stories, legends and histories were the basis of most plays of the time. The story of Romeo and Juliet was a very old one, probably first heard centuries before Shakespeare wrote his version; but the 16th century saw an upsurge of interest in the tale, with the publication of the story in Italian, French and English. It was published in verse form by Arthur Brooke in 1562, and Brooke refers to an earlier play with the same title in his introduction. Shakespeare may have seen this, but as no record of it exists, we cannot know how it may have influenced him. Shakespeare certainly seems to have followed the plot of Brooke's version, but with drastic differences: he turned the rather run-of-the-mill verse of Brooke into the most beautiful lyric poetry ever heard on the English stage up to that time; he developed or invented complex, believable characters, and gave the whole a dramatic structure which, in its brilliance and variety, is hard to equal.

Characterization and play structure

The general outlines of the play's characters have obviously been taken from earlier sources, but Shakespeare gave them a totally new perspective. For example, the Nurse was rounded out into a jolly, loving and quite important character; Mercutio was built up into a character of brilliant individuality; the Friar was changed entirely from being rather sinister to being unworldly, well-meaning and totally sincere; Paris, likewise, became a sympathetic rather than a villainous figure; Juliet was changed from a precocious young woman to an innocent victim of love and tragedy. Shakespeare emphasized the magical, meteoric speed of the love tragedy by compressing the action of the play into a period of five days. By speeding up the pace of the play Shakespeare also underlined the youthful impetuosity of the lovers and their personal tragedy. Above all, he avoided melodrama by making the plot, and particularly the background of the feud, as realistic as the story would allow.

Romeo and Juliet is set in Italy because that is where the story originated, but the setting would be of little interest to Shakespeare's audience. It is doubtful if many, or indeed any, would have visited Italy, and they neither wanted nor expected accuracy of detail. The heat of the day is mentioned, but an English summer can be hot; Juliet refers to a pomegranate tree, but these had been grown in England in recent years; and there are other details giving a vaguely exotic air. The social background of the play is that of England in the late 16th century. The many trees, flowers and animals mentioned were not unknown to the audience and the sea references are topical. The citizens with their clubs in the first scene could easily be London apprentices about to join in a fight, and plague and earthquake had been recently experienced in England. The easy-going Capulet household sounds like that of a typical newly rich London merchant of the time and the religious references are particularly relevant. Reading from books was certainly more of a contemporary interest in this, the century following the invention of printing, than it was during the time when the play was supposed to have been set. All these features are interesting to us, giving us an idea of the preoccupations of Shakespeare's time; they were, in fact, an essential means for Shakespeare to make his story believable and his message understandable to the widest possible audience.

REPUBLIC OF

Lake Garda

Verona

Padua

VENICE

Venice

Marquisate

of

Mantua

River Adige

Mantua

River Po

Duchy of

Ferrara

Ferrara

Adriatic
Sea

Duchy of

Reggio

River Panaro

Modena

MODENA

PAPAL STATES

Bologna

English miles

0   25

VENETIAN REPUBLIC

Milan

Turin

3

2

5

6

Venice

1

4

Bologna

7

Genoa

8

Pisa

10

Florence

Adriatic Sea

Ligurian
Sea

9

Siena

PAPAL STATES

CORSICA
(to Genoa)

Tyrrhenian
Sea

Rome

KINGDOM OF

ITALY

Naples

NAPLES

In the early
16th Century

Key to the States

1 Duchy of Savoy   2 Marquisate of
                            Montferrat

3 Duchy of Milan   8 Republic of Lucca

4 Republic of Genoa   5 Marquisate of Mantua   9 Republic of Siena

6 Duchy of Ferrara   10 Republic of Florence

7 Duchy of Modena

SICILY   Peter McClure 1986

Understanding Romeo and Juliet

An exploration of the major topics and themes in the play

Summaries of themes

Aspects of style

The aspects of style to which your attention is drawn in the commentary are those which in this particular play are most revealing and which are not discussed in detail as themes, images or characters. These aspects include some information about general play structure such as the use of time, the chorus, and some examples of the use of such things as contrast and dramatic irony.

The action of the play was compressed by Shakespeare into five days. If not as continuous as in Greek tragedy, it follows on smoothly and without appreciable time lapse from scene to scene. Although we cannot be sure if the text we have is precisely as Shakespeare wished it, we can still admire the balance of comedy, usually spoken in prose, with more serious drama, usually in poetic form; we can also appreciate the contrasting characters, the sustaining of suspense, the attempt at realistic plotting, and the frequent irony.

Romeo and Juliet has been called a play of contrasts. There are contrasts between characters and between attitudes to love and life. Themes like those of age and youth, love and violence, life and death, and their supporting images are set in opposition to each other. There are even contradictions contained in the images themselves, and the technical term for this is oxymoron. Good examples of oxymoron have been pointed out in the commentary.

Although the tragedy may be caused by fate, the atmosphere of doom is accentuated by the many prophetic utterances of the chief characters. These are ironic because the audience already knows the outcome of the meeting of Romeo and Juliet. The prophecies seem to be only dimly understood by the characters themselves.

Some critics have felt that Chorus makes no essential contribution to the play. They have sometimes argued that Chorus is merely Shakespeare's way of trying to make his play more 'respectable' in the eyes of the literate people of his day, by adding something classical which dated back to the Greeks. It is true that his lines at the beginning of the play summarize the events of the forthcoming Acts; but his appearance at the beginning of the play is important because Shakespeare must have wanted his audience to know *what* was going to happen, so that they could concentrate on *how* it happened and *why* it happened. For example, in a play whose theme is the clash between love and hate, young and old, life and death and the disorder this brings, the Prince is a symbol of order and peace. He speaks strongly enough but he has never been able to halt the feud, and admits at the end that he should have been firmer, and that it is the lovers' deaths, not the power of his authority, that has brought peace.

Imagery

It is, of course, Shakespeare's mastery of language that makes him unique, and to fully appreciate his art, a study of the means he uses to make us see and hear what he wanted us to understand repays the effort. *Romeo and Juliet* predates the four great tragedies of *Hamlet*, *King Lear*, *Macbeth* and *Othello*, and stands separately in that it does not attempt to follow their pattern of classical tragedy. Classical tragedy is a drama in which a person, usually of high social status, is doomed to disaster and death because of one fatal weakness of character. It is true that in *Romeo and Juliet* the themes of fate and death are strong, but there are also overtones of chance, the consequences of passion, the effect of age on youth, and of course the power of love in its many forms. In this tragedy, events and ill luck are as important as character and fate. There is a wealth of imagery: of light, darkness, animals, flowers, the body, the sea, the air. The imagery hovers around the themes. The imagery of the play sometimes strikes us directly with its effects and at other times makes its impact very subtly. The way the images are used in *Romeo and Juliet* is a fine example of the triumph of Shakespeare's art.

However an image can only be effective if its allusion is clearly understood, and therefore it is not surprising that Shakespeare's images often reflect contemporary 16th-century interests. For example, in the previous 100 years books had become more accessible, grammar schools had been founded, and the rising middle class had become more literate. Hence the many references to 'by the book', 'without book', 'Had I it written' for example. In much the same way you will find several allusions to falconry, archery, the Elizabethans' philosophical ideas about the universe and so on. Do not be put off by the strangeness of some of these ideas, or by the sometimes unfamiliar words, but try to see them as reflections of the things which were important or commonplace in a society which was in many ways very different from ours of today.

Age

The conflict between the ideas and feelings of old people and young people is an essential ingredient of the tragedy. It is the younger members of the Montague and Capulet families who have kept the feud going. The slowness of the (older) Friar and Nurse contrasts with the haste of the young lovers. In the end it is the young lovers who, through their deaths, teach the older ones a lesson.

The body

References to the body, and imagery based on it, are frequently present in this play of young and passionate love. The mouth, ears and hands are understandably emphasized in the imagery; but in a play which also deals with violence and death so are the other parts of the body.

Imagery involving food seems very appropriate in the play, since the lovers meet at a feast and Juliet 'dies' while a feast is being prepared. In the same way Juliet 'drinks' Romeo's words, Romeo's wit is 'sharp sauce', honey kills the appetite as violent delights kill those who indulge in them, Juliet's breath is as sweet as honey, and the body needs food as the soul needs love.

Creatures

Animal imagery is always near the surface in Shakespeare's plays. This is largely because of the way Elizabethans tended to look at the world. The current philosophy was that there was a natural order headed by God and the king, in which every person, plant and animal had a natural place and purpose. This notion continually invited people, especially writers, to use comparisons and metaphors, so that beautiful animals were considered the counterpart of good people, while for instance worms and reptiles could be thought of as reflections of foul things in human life.

Darkness and light

Images of darkness stand for death, violence, sorrow and secrecy. Romeo seeks darkness to hide his melancholy at the beginning of the play; the lovers welcome night when they can be safely alone; and the blackness of the tomb and the darkness outside epitomize the tragedy of their deaths.

Light, whiteness or paleness are often used as images of love, life or hope, and also as the opposites of these. Romeo sees Juliet as the sun, brighter than a torch or than the stars. Juliet sees Romeo as whiter than snow. They both fear the light when they lose hope, but even in the tomb Juliet's beauty appears to Romeo to make the darkness light.

Death and sickness

Death is obviously one of the key themes of the play and is introduced within the first few lines. The Prince threatens the brawlers with the death penalty in the first scene and later Romeo dreams of his own death. Death is constantly prophesied and five people actually die violently as part of the plot of the play.

Many situations of distress or wrongdoing are imaged in terms of sickness: the disorder of Verona's feuding society and its 'cankered hate', Romeo's secrecy about Rosaline, 'like a blighted bud', and the urgency of Romeo's love for Juliet, which needs the 'holy physic' of the Friar. Very often the parallel is with disease in plants.

Dreams

More often than not dreams are linked to prophecy and visions in the play. Dreams were probably taken more seriously by ordinary people in Shakespeare's day than they are now, although many people still set great store by them. Romeo takes his dreams very seriously, although he finds it difficult to understand what they may mean. Like the actions of fate Romeo's dreams are, to him, inexplicable. Mercutio, however, in one of the most impressive speeches in the play, sees dreams as things sent to torment men and, anticipating modern psychology, as a sort of wish-fulfilment.

The elements

The use of imagery about the elements, fire, earth and water, is closely related to the workings of fate, since the elements cannot be controlled any more than fate can. The elements are quite neutral: the earth both gives life and accepts the dead; the air may be scornful of Tybalt at one moment, but is sweetened by Juliet's breath the next; the sea is full of unpredictable danger, like life; fire may be the brightness of light, or it may be the hot passion which leads to violence and death. The idea of passion, violence and disorder is connected not only with the 'civil brawls' of the feud, but with the unnaturalness of false love, the violence of angry passions, and also with the confusion in nature when young people can die because of the mistakes of the old.

Fate

Fate is an important theme in the play. From the first mention of the 'star-crossed lovers' we have the feeling that they are doomed through no fault of their own. Romeo feels his future 'hanging in the stars' and that he is 'fortune's fool'. But society and fate also play some part in the tragedy. There is a strong sense of the inevitable about the final resolution which strikes many people when they see or read the play. We could call it a matter of the quirks of fate; there are several occasions where the unfortunate outcome of an event is the result of what we might call bad luck.

Passions

Most of the violence in the play results not so much from hate as from social disorder. Sampson and Gregory only think they ought to fight, Tybalt says he hates but actually only uses the feud as an excuse for his natural physical aggressiveness. Romeo is forced to fight because of his code of honour. Violence of all sorts is in contrast to the peacefulness of the lovers, and is particularly in contrast to Mercutio's wild imagination and Capulet's verbal violence. Violent feelings are only felt by the lovers when society will not leave them alone.

Love is obviously one of the main themes of the play, but it is also a very complex one. Approaches to love vary from the violent and bestial attitudes of Sampson and Gregory, through Romeo's early sadness, Benvolio's idea of suffering, Mercutio's bawdy simplifications, the Nurse's idea of fun, the Capulets' mercenary notions of marriage and wealth, to Romeo and Juliet's final concept of deep, passionate love. The play could be seen as a study in attitudes to love, but the final message seems to be that Romeo and Juliet's true love is the powerful one, because it can conquer hate and even death.

Plants

Many of Shakespeare's audience would be nearer the soil and more knowledgeable about it than we are today, and certainly they had more gardens, orchards and woods in their lives than we do. Like animals, plants were seen as part of the natural order. Also, it was common to compare the world with a garden, and with its many plants: beautiful or ugly, healthy or sick, beneficial or poisonous. A comprehensive idea of how this imagery is used is found in the Friar's first speech.

Sight

In this story of young love, we would expect imagery relating to the eyes to be prominent, and it is therefore not surprising to find that Juliet says early on that she will 'look to love', and that it is Romeo's sight of Juliet that fills him with love. It is Juliet's kinsmen's eyes that Romeo must hide from, and it is love that 'lent' him eyes. Romeo goes to look upon Juliet for the last time in the tomb and says, 'Eyes, look your last'.

Time

What really caused the tragedy is for us, the audience, to decide. Was it fate, the feud, Tybalt, Paris, the breakdown of the Friar's plan, or all these events together? We do know that the speed with which events occur is a contributory factor. The ever-present sense of haste can be seen in the actions of the characters and often also in the imagery of their words.

Analysis chart

Scene reference (Day / Time of day / Act.Scene / Important event / Page in commentary on which scene first occurs)

Act.Scene	Day	Time of day	Important event	Page
1.0	Sunday	—	Capulet and Montague servants fight	16
1.1	Sunday	Morning	Capulet and Paris discuss marriage of Juliet	16
1.2	Sunday	—	Juliet will 'look to like' at the feast	25
1.3	Sunday	Evening	Mercutio's 'Queen Mab' speech	27
1.4	Sunday	Suppertime	Romeo sees Juliet and falls in love	31
1.5	Sunday	—		33
2.0	Sunday	Night		36
2.1	Sunday	Night	Romeo and Juliet exchanges vows of love	36
2.2	Sunday	Night		37
2.3	Monday	Early morning	Romeo asks the Friar to marry him and Juliet	40
2.4	Monday	Morning	Romeo tells the Nurse he will wed Juliet	42
2.5	Monday	Mid-morning		45
2.6	Monday	Afternoon	Romeo and Juliet are married	46
3.1	Monday	—	Tybalt kills Mercutio. Romeo kills Tybalt. Romeo banished	47
3.2	Monday	Evening	Juliet learns of Romeo's banishment	49
3.3	Monday	Late night		51
3.4	Monday	Very late night	Capulet tells Paris Juliet will wed him Thursday	53
3.5	Tuesday	Dawn	Romeo and Juliet part. Juliet will not wed Paris!	53
4.1	Tuesday	—	Friar's cell: only meeting of Juliet and Paris	57
4.2	Tuesday	Evening	Capulet moves wedding to Wednesday	59
4.3	Tuesday	Night	Juliet takes Friar's potion	59
4.4	Wed	—		60
4.5	Wed	Early morning	Nurse discovers Juliet's 'body'	60
5.1	Wed	—	Romeo hears Juliet is dead: visits Apothecary	62
5.2	Thurs	Thurs evening	Friar learns his message didn't get to Romeo	64
5.3	Fri	Night and early morning	Romeo kills Paris, then kills self. Juliet stabs herself	64

Characters and Themes (● = appears / theme present)

Row	1.0	1.1	1.2	1.3	1.4	1.5	2.0	2.1	2.2	2.3	2.4	2.5	2.6	3.1	3.2	3.3	3.4	3.5	4.1	4.2	4.3	4.4	4.5	5.1	5.2	5.3
Characters																										
Benvolio	●			●										●												
Gregory	●																									
Juliet		●	●		●			●	●		●	●			●				●	●		●				●
Lady Capulet		●		●		●								●					●							●
Lady Montague		●																								●
Lord Capulet		●	●			●											●	●	●	●		●	●			●
Lord Montague																										●
Mercutio				●	●			●			●	●		●												
Paris			●	●															●				●			●
Romeo		●	●		●	●		●	●	●			●	●	●	●			●					●		●
Rosaline		●	●																							
Sampson		●																								
The Friar										●			●			●			●	●			●	●	●	●
The Nurse			●			●					●	●				●			●			●	●	●		
Tybalt		●				●								●												
Themes																										
Age		●	●	●		●					●		●					●								●
Aspects of style	●	●	●	●	●	●	●		●	●	●		●	●	●		●	●	●	●		●	●	●	●	●
Creatures		●	●	●	●	●			●		●	●	●	●	●	●			●	●			●			●
Darkness and light		●	●	●	●	●		●	●		●		●	●		●			●		●					●
Death and sickness		●		●		●			●	●				●				●	●		●			●		●
Dreams				●	●				●												●					●
Fate	●	●	●	●		●		●	●	●			●	●		●		●	●		●		●	●	●	●
Passion		●	●	●	●	●		●	●		●			●	●	●			●				●		●	●
Plants		●	●					●	●	●						●			●							●
Sight		●	●	●	●	●											●						●			●
The body		●	●	●	●	●	●	●					●		●	●		●	●			●				●
The elements		●	●					●			●					●			●						●	●
Time		●		●		●		●		●				●	●	●	●		●	●		●	●	●		●
Page in commentary on which scene first occurs	16	16	25	27	31	33	36	36	37	40	42	45	46	47	49	51	53	53	57	59	59	60	60	62	64	64

Finding your way around the commentary

Each page of the commentary gives the following information:

1   A quotation from the start of each paragraph on which a comment is made, or act/scene or line numbers plus a quotation, so that you can easily locate the right place in your text.

2   A series of comments, explaining, interpreting, and drawing your attention to important incidents, characters and aspects of the text.

3   For each comment, headings to indicate the important characters, themes, and ideas dealt with in the comment.

4   For each heading, a note of the comment numbers in this guide where the previous or next comment dealing with that heading occured.

Thus you can use this commentary section in a number of ways.

1   Turn to that part of the commentary dealing with the chapter/act you are perhaps revising for class discussion or essay. Read through the comments in sequence, referring all the time to the text, which you should have open before you. The comments will direct your attention to all the important things of which you should take note.

2   Take a single character or topic from the list on page 14. Note the comment number next to it. Turn to that comment in this guide, where you will find the first of a number of comments on your chosen topic. Study it, and the appropriate part of your text to which it will direct you. Note the comment number in this guide where the next comment for your topic occurs and turn to it when you are ready. Thus, you can follow one topic right through your text. If you have an essay to write on a particular character or theme just follow the path through this guide and you will soon find everything you need to know!

3   A number of relevant relationships between characters and topics are listed on page 15. To follow these relationships throughout your text, turn to the comment indicated. As the previous and next comment are printed at the side of each page in the commentary, it is a simple matter to flick through the pages to find the previous or next occurrence of the relationship in which you are interested.

For example, you want to examine in depth the themes of darkness and light in the play. Turning to the single topic list, you will find that this theme first occurs in comment 29. On turning to comment 29 you will discover a zero (0) in the place of the previous reference (because this is the first time that it has occurred) and the number 38 for the next reference. You now turn to comment 38 and find that the previous comment number is 29 (from where you have just been looking) and that the next reference is to comment 41, and so on throughout the text.

You also wish to trace the relationship between Romeo and Juliet throughout the play. From the relationships list, you are directed to comment 134. This is the first time that both Romeo and Juliet are discussed together and you will find that the next time that this happens occurs in comment 136 (the 'next' reference for both Romeo and Juliet). On to comment 136 and you will now discover that two different comment numbers are given for the subject under examination – numbers 153 and 137. This is because each character is traced separately as well as together and you will have to continue tracing them separately until you finally come to comment 225 – the next occasion on which both Romeo and Juliet are discussed.

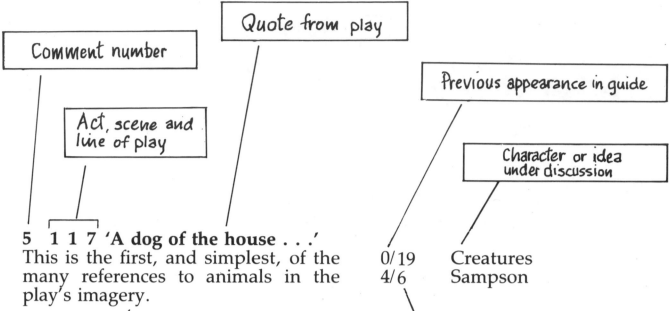

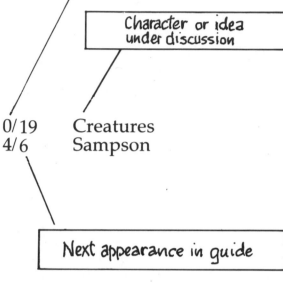

5 1 1 7 'A dog of the house . . .'
This is the first, and simplest, of the many references to animals in the play's imagery.

0/19   Creatures
4/6   Sampson

Single topics:

	Comment no:		Comment no:
Aspects of style	1	Benvolio	18
Age	32	Lord Capulet	26
Creatures	5	Lady Capulet	24
Darkness and light	29	The Friar	176
Death and sickness	20	Gregory	11
Dreams	97	Sampson	4
The elements	22	Juliet	6
Fate	2	Mercutio	85
Passion	7	Lord Montague	403
Plants	33	Lady Montague	24
Sight	21	The Nurse	84
Time	4	Paris	63
The body	10	Romeo	36
		Rosaline	58
		Tybalt	19

Relationships:

			Comment no:
Aspects of style	and	Darkness and light	38
		Death and sickness	159
		Fate	2
		Passion	35
		The body	135
		The Friar	176
Passion	and	Darkness and light	70
		Death and sickness	150
		Juliet	102
		Lady Capulet	99
		Mercutio	85
		Plants	148
		Romeo	43
		The body	12
		The elements	35
The body	and	Age	121
		Juliet	68
		Mercutio	114
		Romeo	126
		Sampson	10
Romeo	and	Creatures	125
		Darkness and light	41
		Death and sickness	59
		Fate	75
		Juliet	134
		Sight	126
		The elements	44
Juliet	and	Creatures	171
		Darkness and light	102
		Death and sickness	139
		The Nurse	84
		Time	89
Mercutio	and	Creatures	114
		Dreams	114
		The Nurse	85
The Friar	and	Fate	189
		Plants	176
		Time	190
Death and sickness	and	Darkness and light	150
		The body	182
Passion	and	The elements	35
		The Nurse	85
Paris	and	Fate	63

Commentary

Prologue

1 0 0 1 'Two households . . .'
In Greek tragedy, the Chorus was a kind of narrator who commented on the action of the play from time to time. Here, the Chorus gives the audience the basic facts of the feud and how the death of the lovers ends it. The audience now knows what the characters do not, and can interpret their actions accordingly. Here the language of the Chorus is in the form of a sonnet, which adds formal dignity to what is said.

0/2   Aspects
of style

2 0 0 5 'From forth the fatal loins . . .'
Fate causes the tragedy, not the actions of people. This idea goes back to ancient Greek drama.

References to 'star-crossed', 'death-marked', 'fatal loins' and so on would immediately catch the attention of an Elizabethan audience. Modern audiences too are fascinated not so much by *what* will happen (because most people will already know how the story ends) but with the *way* it will happen.

1/3   Aspects
of style
0/51   Fate

Act 1

3 1 1 1 'Gregory, on my word . . .'
In a play which is full of contrasting atmospheres and emotions, we are presented with the first contrast – between the noble poetry of the Chorus and the often vulgar prose of Gregory and Sampson. The puns continue thick and fast with 'colliers' (a term of abuse), 'collier', 'choler' and 'collar' (hangman's type).

Although the servants are armed and ready for trouble, the play starts like a comedy. Word-play, puns and 'quibbles' might be expected from comic characters but they are used by nearly every character in this play, on even the most serious occasions. They represent a literary form which was much admired in Shakespeare's day and which he raised to the height of subtlety.

2/6   Aspects
of style

4 1 1 5 'I strike quickly . . .'
This introduces the idea of impetuous action which will doom the lovers. Notice Sampson's boastful character.

0/5   Sampson
0/13   Time

5 1 1 7 'A dog of the house . . .'
This is the first, and simplest, of the many references to animals in the play's imagery.

0/19   Creatures
4/6   Sampson

Characters and ideas previous/next comment

6 1 1 14 ''Tis true; and therefore women . . .'

3/8 Aspects of style
5/9 Sampson
0/65 Juliet

We should be conscious of an irony in Sampson's words. To 'take to the wall' was to keep to the cleaner side of the footpath, nearer the wall. In what way might it be true that in the play the women are forced to the wall, out of the way, or to extremes? How true is it that the women prove to be the 'weaker vessels'? Study Juliet's determination and resolve in Act 5; contrast her with Lady Capulet.

It would be difficult not to agree that Juliet is forced to extreme actions later in the play, but does this mean she was strong? Maybe she did not have the strength of character to confront the situation directly, and argue it out with her parents. Was she running away from the problem, or were her actions heroic?

Would our attitudes to what she does be different if it had been Romeo who acted as she did, and it was she who was banished? Lady Capulet does seem to be forced 'out of the way' by the men in the play; her husband appears very authoritarian with both his daughter and his wife. But it is she who cries for revenge over the body of Tybalt in Act 3, and her cutting words to her husband in Act 1 show that she is not really too afraid of him.

---

7 1 1 16 '. . . will push Montague's men from the wall . . .'

0/9 Passion

Love, in its broadest sense of the man/woman relationship, is one of the main themes of the play. In Sampson's rape fantasy, love is reduced to the brutal conquest of another's body, to the 'cutting-off' of virginity. Sampson's view of life is corrupted by his hatred, just as Romeo's early infatuation with Rosaline distorts his vision of the world around him. This is in keeping with the Elizabethan view that any kind of extreme of passion makes people 'out of humour', or ill.

---

8 1 1 20 ''Tis all one.'

6/16 Aspects of style

The Elizabethan view of the universe often connected seemingly unrelated or opposite things such as love and hate, hot and cold, fire and water, gold and lead. They saw everything as part of one whole Creation. They thought of the universe as being in a delicate balance which could be upset by man, who was the only agent with free will apart from God.

---

9 1 1 21 '. . . I have fought with the men . . .'

7/12 Passion
6/10 Sampson

Interestingly, although Gregory is spoken to twice by name, the audience is never told Sampson's name. Is it ironic that Sampson should be the one to speak of heads and cutting things off? (Hint: think about a story in the Bible.)

Sampson seems to represent only one aspect of a mature personality. Can you find any other one-dimensional character like him? (Look for help in the summaries of characters on page 71.)

---

10 1 1 22 '. . . maids – I will cut off their heads.'

9/11 Sampson
0/12 The body

References to the human body are frequent in the play, but notice how different characters use them. Sampson is connected with the feud, and his character has a wide streak of animal savagery in it. Such characters use the most bawdy bodily imagery and references. Compare Sampson with Tybalt for example, or with Mercutio. In this particular example in Act 1, Sampson's obscene sexual references appear in marked contrast to the idealized love spoken of later by Romeo and Paris, and even more so to the mature love which develops between Romeo and Juliet. Notice how Romeo,

Paris and Juliet use references to the body in their imagery. Both Sampson and Gregory have violent attitudes towards sexual love; for them love has become hate, and this is their link with the thematic structure of the play.

---

11   1 1 29 '. . .'tis known I am a pretty piece of flesh.'
Sampson is the boastful one, Gregory the quicker thinking one who can cut his partner down to size. Do they ever appear without each other? Are they the two incomplete halves of a whole character?

0/14	Gregory
10/14	Sampson

---

12   1 1 30 ''Tis well thou art not fish; . . .'
References to 'naked weapon', 'maidenheads' and here 'tool', emphasize the physical and sometimes brutal side of love. This notion is developed later through the characters of Mercutio and the Nurse and forms an effective contrast to the other kinds of love seen in the play. There is the fatherly love of Capulet for his daughter; the Nurse cherishes Juliet as her wet-nurse (but can indulge in bawdy sexual repartee with the men when it suits her); the Friar shows fatherly care for the young lovers; and so on. There are many different kinds of 'love' illustrated in the play, and those mentioned above are only a few of them – try making a list of all the types you can identify.

9/23	Passion
10/14	The body

---

13   1 1 30 'Draw thy tool.'
Amidst a whirl of animal and sexual references, Sampson and Gregory encounter their deadly enemies. Striking, thrusting and running have already been mentioned in this scene. The language throughout the play is often used to underpin the general tone and atmosphere. The speed with which fighting breaks out prepares us for the way haste and speed play a large part in the coming tragedy. Notice that the feuding in the play begins with the servants. This points to the degree to which chaos has spread through the society of Verona by distancing it, initially, from the heads of the two houses.

4/22	Time

---

14   1 1 32 'My naked weapon is out.'
Sampson reinforces the previous sexual imagery with his reference to 'naked weapon'. After all his boasting, it would seem by Gregory's implication that Sampson is in fact a coward. Is his name a joke?

11/17	Gregory
11/15	Sampson
12/15	The body

---

15   1 1 41 'Nay, as they dare.'
Sampson introduces the imagery of the mouth – here to make a provocative and insulting gesture. Study the way the imagery of the mouth, of eating and of devouring is used in the play.

14/17	Sampson
14/68	The body

---

16   1 1 43 'Do you bite your thumb at us, sir?'
This farcical quarrelling which ends in stalemate at line 56 is only revived when Gregory and Sampson see Tybalt. What does this tell you about the feud and about Tybalt's part in keeping it going? Is there any more feuding after Tybalt is killed? Consider whether it matters that we never discover what the feud is about.

8/25	Aspects of style

---

17   1 1 61 'Draw, if you be men.'
Sampson seems to fight only reluctantly. It would appear that Gregory may be the more aggressive of the two, after all, if Sampson is a coward at heart.

14/0	Gregory
15/0	Sampson

---

*Characters and ideas
previous/next comment*

18 1 1 63 'Part, fools!'
The first words of Benvolio sum up his character: the sensible peacemaker. Benvolio translates as 'good will' in Shakespeare's Italian. His is an appropriate name for Mercutio's counterpart. A similar sort of thing occurs in *Twelfth Night*, with the name of the 'ill-willed' character Malvolio.

0/34 Benvolio

19 1 1 65 'What, art thou drawn . . .'
The hind is a female deer. The pun here suggests that they (the men) are hiding amongst women and are therefore cowards. This continues the unflattering view of women introduced by Sampson earlier in the scene.

5/28 Creatures
0/20 Tybalt

20 1 1 66 'Turn thee, Benvolio, look upon thy death.'
Tybalt makes the first mention of death in the play since the Chorus introduced the theme. Think about the sort of character he is, and consider whether it is purely accidental that he introduces this theme into the action, rather than somebody else.

Tybalt's name comes from the Medieval story of 'Reynard the Fox', where he is a cat. This explains Mercutio's jibes of 'Prince of cats' (Act 2), 'rat-catcher' (Act 3), and 'King of cats' (Act 3). It also explains Mercutio's wry reference to his own fatal wound as a 'scratch'. Notice how the names of the characters who are friends in the play end gently with soft 'o' sounds—Romeo, Mercutio, Benvolio; whilst those of the outsiders sound harsh—Tybalt, Paris.

0/33 Death and sickness
19/22 Tybalt

21 1 1 66 'Turn thee, Benvolio, look upon they death.'
Notice how the first introduction of the theme of death (since the Chorus) at once connects it with sight. The idea of 'if looks could kill . . .' occurs again later in the play, in connection with Romeo and Juliet

0/79 Sight

22 1 1 69 'What, drawn, and talk of peace?'
By this point two more contrasting characters have been introduced into the action of the play. Tybalt rushes into the fray and his impetuousness will cause disaster, although so will that of other characters later on. Tybalt hates hell, he hates peace and he hates Montagues—he is one of the constant factors in the play, whose character neither develops nor reveals other sides. He is a perpetually excitable and angry fellow.

0/31 The elements
13/40 Time
20/127 Tybalt

23 1 1 72 'Clubs, bills and partisans!'
The general citizenry are equally against both Capulets and Montagues. Their feud is a constant running sore in society—hence Escalus's concern. At this point in the play we see Capulet enter in his nightgown. The day began with civil disorder, which was connected to domestic disorder through the involvement of the servants. Soon we will see personal disorder, when Romeo sees himself very much as a soul in torment.

12/35 Passion

24 1 1 75 'What noise is this?'
Capulet and Montague go through the motions of joining the fight. What does Lady Capulet's remark show about her attitude to both her husband and the feud? Is Lady Montague's attitude any different? Notice how the two ladies are being used to point to and contrast with the action in the play and the themes which are being developed.

0/88 Lady Capulet
0/397 Lady Montague

	Characters and ideas previous/next comment

25   1 1 76 'A crutch, a crutch!'
A strong theme in the play is the contrast between the feelings and attitudes of the young and those of the old. For example notice how Lady Capulet calls for a crutch in opposition to her husband's call for a sword. This ridicules the foolishness of the feud between two old men. The idea of age is introduced and the human body is shown as a victim of the passage of time. The world of Romeo and Juliet is one of youth overruled by age.

16/27   Aspects of style

26   1 1 77 'My sword, I say!'
Although an old man, Capulet is still keen to get into a brawl. Or is this just for show? Notice how Capulet is very subdued over the body of Tybalt later on, when it is Lady Capulet who desires revenge.

0/62   Lord Capulet

27   1 1 81 'Rebellious subjects . . .'
The order of appearance of the characters so far has been: Capulet's servants, Montague's servants, Benvolio, Tybalt, the Capulets, the Montagues, the Prince. What is interesting about this is that two important characters have not even been mentioned yet; what do you think is the dramatic significance of this? Characters and themes are introduced in an elegant symmetry, with one factor carefully balancing another, until all the main themes have been introduced. This produces strong dramatic tension, held in balance. The introduction of Romeo and Juliet, and their love, is the catalyst. This final ingredient produces a chain reaction. The Prince appears only three times in the play. On every occasion his dramatic function is the same. What therefore does he represent and symbolize in the play?

25/30   Aspects of style

28   1 1 83 'Will they not hear?'
Those who should show wisdom and leadership are criticized by the Prince, who likens their savagery to that of beasts. Their bloodlust is linked through the imagery to the theme of fire, and the recurring image of 'bloody hands' is introduced into the play.

19/46   Creatures

29   1 1 83 'What, ho–you men, you beasts . . .'
Compare the way fire imagery is used here with the way Romeo and Juliet use the imagery of light.

0/38   Darkness and Light

30   1 1 86 'On pain of torture . . .'
The prince is concerned about the effect the two families' pointless feud is having on society. He is fulfilling the accepted role of the monarch in Elizabethan society. The Prince's name Escalus derives from the Italian 'della scala' meaning 'of the scales', or 'justice'. The family name of the famous rulers of Verona was della Scala, and it was in the time of Bartolomeo della Scala in the 14th century that historians had placed the original story of Romeo and Julietta.

27/35   Aspects of style

31   1 1 87 'Throw your mistempered weapons . . .'
Escalus's comment is nicely ambiguous; it is equally they, as well as their weapons which are mistempered and disordered. Their pointless fighting causes chaos in society.

22/35   The elements

32   1 1 92 'And made Verona's ancient citizens . . .'
The idea of old people being incapable of coping with the problems of youth is introduced very early on in the play. Age is linked to 'cankered hate', which is an idea frequently used in the play. Notice which other themes are developed in parallel to these.

0/62	Age

33   1 1 95 'Cankered with peace . . .'
The image of diseased plants is used several times, as here, to illustrate unhappy or 'sick' emotions.

20/46	Death and sickness
0/39	Plants

34   1 1 106 'Here were the servants . . .'
Notice how neatly and accurately Benvolio relates the previous incident. Shakespearian drama often uses characters like this, as a sort of mini-chorus to keep everybody in the audience up to date with what has happened.

18/37	Benvolio

35   1 1 109 'The fiery Tybalt . . .'
The qualities of fire have much in common with the uncontrollable nature of rage. Similarly, the elements, like fate, cannot be controlled by man. Tybalt cannot harm the wind. Benvolio uses the imagery of hissing and breathing about the 'fiery Tybalt', and this reflects the situation very effectively. Tybalt's name is derived from Tybert the cat – hence the word we use today: 'tibby'. The emphasis on word-sounds is something which you will find throughout the play, and not only in the puns. You will need to listen for it carefully because when we read a play, as opposed to watching it performed, such things can be easily missed.

30/38	Aspects of style
23/43	Passion
31/44	The elements

36   1 1 116 'O where is Romeo?'
This is the first mention of Romeo. He is depicted as the much-loved son of a woman whose family seems to be her whole life.

0/37	Romeo

37   1 1 118 'Madam, an hour before the worshipped sun . . .'
Contrast this speech of Benvolio with his previous one, and with the one which follows. The speech at this point suddenly becomes poetic and we notice that Benvolio's only really lyrical speech introduces us to Romeo. Notice how the atmosphere of conflict disappears with the introduction of his name. The device used to inject Romeo into the action of the play is also used again later at the Capulet feast, but with a different speaker.

34/48	Benvolio
36/39	Romeo

38   1 1 118 'Madam, an hour before the worshipped sun . . .'
The first mention of Romeo is preceded by descriptions of sunlight, references to worshipping and silence. This imagery accompanies Romeo and Juliet throughout the play. So also, as we might expect, does the opposite imagery.

35/42	Aspects of style
29/41	Darkness and light

39   1 1 121 'Where, underneath the grove of sycamore . . .'
The sycamore was traditionally associated with disappointed lovers, and its name is probably being used here as a pun: 'sick amour'.

33/65	Plants
37/40	Romeo

*Characters and ideas
previous/next comment*

40   1 1 130 'And gladly shunned who gladly fled from me.'
Romeo is depicted here as an impetuous, elusive shadow. Frequent touches
like this, which associate Romeo with haste and speed, strengthen the
impression of his headlong rush to destruction.

39/41	Romeo
22/66	Time

---

41   1 1 131 'Many a morning hath he there been seen . . .'
Montague becomes lyrical when introducing us to Romeo. Whereas
Romeo's love for Juliet will be associated with light, this unrequited love for
Rosaline makes him seek out the dark. Dawn and light are here associated
with solitude and darkness, just as the human face becomes associated with
the heavens during the course of the play. This cloud of images follows
Romeo and Juliet through the play, emphasizing their destiny. Compare
these early references with their parting scene at dawn (Act 2, scene 2) to see
how the imagery develops.

38/60	Darkness and light
40/42	Romeo

---

42   1 1 136 'The shady curtains from Aurora's bed . . .'
Aurora was a goddess of the dawn, married to Tithonus, whose 'bed' she was
supposed to leave each morning. This is the first of numerous references to
mythology in the play. Elizabethan audiences would be more familiar with
classical literature, mythology and the Bible than today's audience is. Such
references, and those based on superstitions, are always associated with
Romeo or Juliet, nobody else.

38/47	Aspects of style
41/43	Romeo

---

43   1 1 137 'Away from light steals home my heavy son . . .'
Romeo has made for himself an 'artificial night'. In what way is his love-
sickness for Rosaline artificial? Montague is afraid that this sickness will do
Romeo harm. This is ironic because it is later replaced by something far more
dangerous; real love for Juliet. This love eventually locks 'fair daylight' out in
a very literal way (the tomb). The play can be seen as a subtle study of what
is 'artificial' with Shakespeare using the play to portray artificiality of
character, of speech, and of values. Is there anything or anyone in the play
which represents the world of the 'real' and genuine?

35/48	Passion
42/44	Romeo

---

44 1 1 141 'Black and portentous must this humour prove . . .'
The Elizabethans thought that man's passions had to be ruled by reason if
social and natural disorder were to be avoided. Love-sickness was therefore
seen as being both an emotional and a medical problem.

43/47	Romeo
35/45	The elements

---

45   1 1 150 'So far from sounding and discovery . . .'
Images of sailing, of unchartered waters and of measuring depths or
'sounding', especially of one's own character, are common in Shakespeare,
and recur at important points in *Romeo and Juliet*.

44/50	The elements

---

46   1 1 151 'As is the bud bit . . .
Study Montague's imagery – the biting mouth of an 'envious worm'
destroying a bud's promise of beauty. The 'envious worm' is an early use of
an image which eventually becomes that of the worms in the tomb. Later in
the play this idea is also developed into the vision of death's mouth (the
tomb) devouring Juliet and Romeo.

28/78	Creatures
33/52	Death and sickness

47 1 1 164 'Not having that which having makes them short.'
Romeo speaks an ironic truth; joy will soon shorten his 'hours' in a tragic way.

42/49	Aspects of style
44/49	Romeo

48 1 1 169 'Alas that love, so gentle in his view . . .'
This is a more aristocratic view of love than that of Sampson or Gregory. To be in love here is to suffer torment – which was a common idea in Elizabethan England, and one found a lot in the love poetry of the period.

37/104	Benvolio
43/49	Passion

49 1 1 176 'Why then, O brawling love, O loving hate . . .'
Romeo shares Benvolio's views about love, and his contradicting images express his emotional disorder. The grouping together of opposites, which we see at this point in the play, is known as oxymoron. It is used here to highlight the very real contradictions in the play, where life is seen as death, and death as life. Notice how, a few lines further on, Romeo talks about 'still-waking sleep, that is not what it is'. This seems like a vision of the future – a vision of the tomb.

47/53	Aspect of style
48/50	Passion
47/50	Romeo

50 1 1 190 'Love is a smoke made with . . .'
Romeo's fanciful imagery of fire and water seems rather forced and artificial here. By using so many different descriptions for his passion, Romeo shows us that he is in love with the idea of being in love, rather than actually being in love with another real person. Notice how we never see Rosaline, and Romeo never meets her on stage although she is invited to the Capulets. Romeo's language is artificial and intellectual, rather than sincere and passionate. The use of rhyming couplets makes the speech sound more like a well-rehearsed recitation, rather than a revelation of inner torment. Compare this with his use of imagery when he first sees Juliet, when we can see a much less ornate use of words.

49/53	Passion
49/54	Romeo
45/51	The elements

51 1 1 192 'Being vexed, a sea nourished with . . .'
The sea imagery depicts the ocean as a powerful and fickle element, like fate. The inability of man to control or influence either of them strengthens the pervasive atmosphere in the play, where we sometimes might sense that events take their headlong course irrespective of the actions of the individuals involved. In this respect, Shakespeare's rather heavy (some would say too heavy) use of coincidence could be said to be essential. Coincidence can only be attributed to fate or destiny.

2/55	Fate
50/72	The elements

52 1 1 202 'Bid a sick man in sadness make his will.'
To Romeo, illness and even death are strongly associated with the feelings of love which he is suffering.

46/59	Death and sickness

53 1 1 206 'A right good markman.'
Images associated with archery can be found in many parts of the play; usually as we might expect, in connection with Cupid. The example here is to do with being successful in love.

49/56	Aspects of style
50/54	Passion

*Characters and ideas
previous/next comment*

54   1 1 208 'Well, in that hit you miss.'
Romeo seems almost to admire Rosaline's firmness of purpose, which makes his love so hopeless and he revels in melancholy. Rosaline's love is unattainable, and therefore Romeo's prospects are hopeless. Suffering unrequited love was a fashionable malady in intellectual circles at the time. Today we might see it as a rather immature sort of love, but the Elizabethans took it fairly seriously.

53/57	Passion
50/56	Romeo

55   1 1 208 'Well, in that hit you miss.'
Often in Shakespeare's plays the thing we most regret in a particular character is also the thing we most admire in them. For example, in the case of Romeo this might be his desire for ideal love; unrealistic, uncompromising, even fatal, but wonderful. Try to think what kinds of thing might fall into this category for some of the other characters in the play, like Mercutio for instance.

51/63	Fate

56   1 1 209 'With Cupid's arrow. She hath Dian's wit . . .'
Zeus was supposed to have conquered the chaste Diana, the goddess of the Moon, by entering her bedchamber in the form of a shower of gold. This reference was probably meant to be a compliment to Queen Elizabeth I, who was noted for the pride she took in her virginity.

53/61	Aspects of style
54/57	Romeo

57   1 1 216 'That, when she dies, with beauty dies her store.'
Rosaline's 'store' of beauty will not be passed on through children – she will die chaste. This notion is a constantly recurring theme in Shakespeare's sonnets, and Romeo appears to be in love with the same romantic 'dark lady' who features in them, rather than with a real woman.

54/64	Passion
56/59	Romeo

58   1 1 223 'She hath forsworn to love; . . .'
Rosaline seems to have made the same vow of chastity which a nun makes. There seems to be no reason to think she is heartless or callous, although Romeo interprets it that way. Is he just feeling sorry for himself? Notice the contrast between Rosaline's forswearing-to-love and Juliet's looking-to-like speech. Rosaline and Juliet are interesting characters to compare.

0/77	Rosaline

59   1 1 224 'Do I live dead that live to tell it now.'
It is ironic that Romeo continues to associate love with death. The strength of his feelings will eventually lead to his death, and this is something for which the play consistently prepares us.

52/90	Death and sickness
57/74	Romeo

60   1 1 230 'These happy masks that kiss fair ladies' brows . . .'
Imagery to do with sight is used to emphasize the idea that blackness and night are also linked to fairness, beauty and light.

41/70	Darkness and light

61   1 1 235 'What doth her beauty serve but as a note . . .'
This is only one of several references to reading from books in the play. Can you think why Shakespeare might have thought such imagery appropriate, bearing in mind the period when the play was written? Read 'Aspects of style' on page 8 for more information on this.

56/72	Aspects of style

62 1 2 3 'For men so old as we to keep the peace.'
The conflict of attitudes between youth and age occurs frequently in the play. Here it is suggested that it is the young who keep the feud going. Is there any truth at all in this accusation? Look at the first meeting of Capulet and Montague – it is possible to see that perhaps at least one of them is not all that keen to continue the feud.

32/83	Age
26/68	Lord Capulet

63   1 2 4 'Of honourable reckoning are you both, . . .'
The plot begins to develop some new twists here. The presence of Paris, and his mission, will produce tragic complications for Romeo and Juliet. Some critics have argued that there is too much use of coincidence, luck and chance in the play – they think it makes the play too 'artificial'. For example, does it matter that it is purely coincidence that Paris happens to be seeking Juliet's hand in marriage at this particular time?

55/75	Fate
0/64	Paris

64   1 2 6 'But now, my lord, what say you to my suit?'
Paris is different from Romeo – not opposite, just different. Paris is calm and well mannered and speaks to Capulet about his love for Juliet. Romeo, on the other hand, who cannot speak to Capulet because of the feud, speaks only to Juliet of his love. Paris is the one who represents the normal and expected form of Elizabethan courtship.

63/67	Paris
57/67	Passion

65   1 2 10 'Let two more summers wither . . .'
The imagery of plant decay and ripening is used to denote the passage of time, and the need for care and nourishment if a crop is to reach maturity and harvest. Rather ominously, Juliet's 'ripeness' to wed is talked of in the same breath as 'withering'. Can you recall Montague's reference to the 'bud bit with an envious worm'? Who was he talking about? Look at scene 1 in this Act. Montague's meaning was that Romeo was struck down with a blight, which would stop him reaching maturity. Such connections between images in the play are not accidental. Imagery is the poetic skeleton of Shakespearian drama, through which the plot acts on our emotions.

6/68	Juliet
33/71	Plants

66   1 2 10 'Let two more summers wither . . .'
Capulet's attitude here is very different from the one he shows a little later on, when Juliet cannot be married quickly enough for him. Similarly, Paris's comment about 'happy mothers' is echoed almost word for word by Lady Capulet in the next scene, in spite of Capulet's opposition to the idea here. What dramatic effect do you think these reversals of attitude prepare us for? They are pre-echoes in miniature of the reversal of other situations, such as the obedient Juliet's rebellion, her mock-death, and the proposition that surface values must be jettisoned to preserve what really matters.

40/89	Time

67   1 2 12 'Younger than she are happy mothers made.'
This is another view of love; that a woman is fulfilled, not by the passion of love, but by the calmer pleasures of motherhood.

64/100	Paris
64/70	Passion

68   1 2 14 'Earth hath swallowed all my hopes but she; . . .'
The literal meaning is that his other children are dead and buried, but the image of the earth swallowing them produces an impression that fate is invincible, and indeed at the end of the play we see the imagery of the mouth reach its greatest power in the atmosphere of the tomb. The 'hopeful lady of my earth' sounds charming, and we warm to Capulet. But is he really

65/84	Juliet
62/69	Lord Capulet
15/76	The body

thinking of Juliet or only of his own ambitions for her? Is he really considering her 'consent' or is this his way of making her seem more precious and therefore more desirable to Paris?

---

69   1 2 24 'At my poor house . . .'
Is this the false modesty of the rich? He is, after all, described as 'the great rich Capulet' by the servant later in the scene. Is Capulet sincere or is he 'artificial' in the sense that Romeo's love for Rosaline was artificial?

68/70	Lord Capulet

---

70   1 2 25 'Earth-treading stars that make dark heaven light.'
The brightness of stars is associated with young women – the objects of love. This emphasizes the connection between heavenly things and events here on earth, which was a common Elizabethan idea and one frequently found in Shakespeare's plays.

60/80	Darkness and light
69/71	Lord Capulet
67/73	Passion

---

71   1 2 29 'Among fresh female buds shall you this night . . .'
Here the buds of spring symbolize young womanhood. The connection between plants and youth is made again and again in the play. What do you think could be the dramatic effect of this? Plants and youth are related through early and vigorous growth, uncontaminated by the canker of old age. Both have an innocence and charm as they ripen.

70/129	Lord Capulet
65/74	Plants

---

72   1 2 38 'Find them out whose names are written here!'
The 'comic servant' breaks into two passages of lyric poetry, in his contrasting prose. His examples of disorder are reminiscent of Romeo's speech about love in the previous scene: 'heavy lightness, serious vanity'.

61/77	Aspects of style
51/73	The elements

---

73   1 2 45 'Tut, man, one fire burns out another's burning.'
Love is likened by Benvolio to fire, pain and grief, which can apparently only be relieved by more pain and grief! The suggestion is that one extreme can be cancelled by another. This is a prophetic remark, because a kind of fire will actually consume Romeo

70/74	Passion
72/117	The elements

---

74   1 2 51 'Your plantain leaf is excellent for that.'
Romeo mocks Benvolio. A 'plantain leaf' (dock leaf) was used for minor ills and scratches. Romeo feels that he is in need of more powerful medicine. Notice how skilfully this image is made to grow from Benvolio's 'infection to thy eye'. If Romeo were really so burdened with genuine love, do you think he would be able to joke so easily with the servant?

73/79	Passion
71/100	Plants
59/75	Romeo

---

75   1 2 57 'Whipped and tormented and – Good-e'en, good fellow.'
It may be an acceptable piece of dramatic licence that the servant chances to meet Benvolio and Romeo, but how far can we accept the coincidence of Romeo reading the list of guests for him and deciding to go to the feast? The servant, who *happens* to be illiterate, *happens* to meet Romeo. Romeo just *happens*, for no apparent reason, to change his mind and read the list. Such is the degree to which chance and fortune work in this play. Romeo's reference to 'fortune' is ironic in view of whom he meets at the feast. How many of these 'coincidences' would be noticed during an actual stage performance, do you think? Most audiences are in fact unaware of them as such, seeing them as the legitimate acts of fate – and therefore perfectly believable. Romeo

63/119	Fate
74/80	Romeo

suggests that it is his fate to be unhappy. The servant replies that it may be his own fault. Which of them do you think is right?

---

76   1 2 79 'Montagues, I pray come and crush a cup of wine.'
Notice as you study the play how Shakespeare uses the imagery of drinking.

| 68/92 | The body |

---

77   1 2 81 'At this same ancient feast of Capulet's . . .'
Romeo and Benvolio speak to each other in verse, whilst the servant speaks in prose, as is appropriate to his lower status. Noble characters often use prose when speaking to, or about, 'lower' things. Rosaline is mentioned for the first time. Shakespeare introduces incidents not mentioned by the Chorus, and perhaps thereby deliberately surprises the audience, who thought they already knew the plot.

| 72/78 | Aspects of style |
| 58/0 | Rosaline |

---

78   1 2 86 'And I will make thee think thy swan a crow.'
Throughout the play humans are compared with the plant and animal world. Here the elegant white swan is contrasted with the plain black crow. Benvolio's prediction does in fact come true. The words 'swan' and 'crow' are another subtle reminder to us of the other parallels between light and dark and death and life which are woven into the play.

| 77/82 | Aspects of style |
| 46/86 | Creatures |

---

79   1 2 87 'When the devout religion of mine eye . . .'
Romeo takes up the idea of sight, one of the senses, as being important to love. He elaborates on the image with the notion of an 'all-seeing sun'. Benvolio takes up the image, suggesting that Romeo is blinded by Rosaline. Romeo says that when he no longer worships Rosaline, then his tears will turn to fire and consume him as an 'heretic'. It is ironic that his true love for Juliet will indeed 'consume' him, but what could be 'heretical' about his final deed? (Hint: think about how the Church would have regarded his behaviour.)

| 74/81 | Passion |
| 21/126 | Sight |

---

80   1 2 91 'One fairer than my love?'
Rosaline is characterized by Romeo in terms of the bright, hot passion of the sun. What qualities of light and heat does Juliet seem to evoke? Look at the 'garden scene' in Act 2.

| 70/81 | Darkness and light |
| 75/106 | Romeo |

---

81   1 2 95 'But in that crystal scales let there be weighed . . .'
Benvolio's suggestion of beauty and love 'shining' echoes Capulet's image of 'earth-treading stars' earlier in the scene. Echoes such as these are frequent and they maintain the continuity of the imagery. This is a particularly noticeable feature of this play. The symmetry of the play becomes apparent again when Juliet goes to see Paris, and Romeo goes to see Rosaline. Romeo will indeed 'rejoice in splendour' later on, but not in the way he presently thinks.

| 80/103 | Darkness and light |
| 79/85 | Passion |

---

82   1 3 1 'Nurse, where's my daughter?'
This scene contrasts with the last two, in being about the world of the women in the play. Lady Capulet seems to represent the rather artificial and formal side of society, whilst the Nurse represents a more natural and

| 78/84 | Aspects of style |

informal one. Notice how this difference between 'high' and 'low' status is reflected in the subject matter and style of their speech.

---

83   1 3 2 'Now, by my maidenhead at twelve year old, . . .'
The whole of the human body's age is either represented or commented upon in this scene from the infant, to girlhood, motherhood and then through to the Nurse's old age.

62/96	Age

---

84   1 3 2 'Now, by my maidenhead at twelve year old, . . .'
It seems somewhat surprising that Juliet should have grown up as she has, given that she has been raised by a scurrilous and bawdy Nurse. But the characters in the play, although often very individualistic, are not real people and we must be careful not to assume that their behaviour is always subject to the sort of interpretation that we might apply to actual people in the real world. Their purposes are dramatic ones, and we must remember that they have to be understood in those terms.

This calling of Juliet by the Nurse is paralleled at the start of Act 4, in scene 5. There are other structural echoes like this in the play, and you should try to spot them, for they underpin the plot and the actions of the characters.

82/95	Aspects of style
68/87	Juliet
0/85	The Nurse

---

85   1 3 2 'Now, by my maidenhead at twelve year old, . . .'
The Nurse's comment has a sexual connotation, and we find this quite often in her conversation. Her humour is broad but, unlike that of Sampson in the first scene, is not designed as a vehicle for offensiveness. The suggestion she makes here, as a joke at her own expense, is that by the age of 13 she was no longer a virgin. As a character in the action of the play she is Juliet's adviser. However, both she and Mercutio have an important structural role in the play. The bawdy jokes and the emphasis on physical lust act as an important balance to the rather idealized love of Romeo and Juliet and the formal and rather artificial speeches of Paris.

The Nurse is based on the stock figure of the obscene old woman, common in earlier plays of the period. Here the cliché has been much developed, and we find her blessed with the name of Angelica – a delightful piece of wry humour on Shakespeare's part. The irony is continued by Capulet, who calls her 'Lady Wisdom' and 'Good Prudence' in Act 3 scene 5. The name 'Angelica' itself is derived from the Greek 'angelos', meaning messenger, from which we get 'angel'. Angelica is also a herb used in medicine and cookery – an interesting link with the uses of plant imagery in the play.

0/107	Mercutio
81/93	Passion
84/86	The Nurse

---

86   1 3 3 'I bade her come. What, lamb! What, ladybird! – . . .'
To her old foster-nurse the young Juliet is still a little lamb. Romeo will soon be comparing her to a dove.

78/109	Creatures
85/88	The Nurse

---

87   1 3 5 'How now? Who calls?'
There might be several dramatic reasons why Shakespeare keeps back the appearance of Juliet for so long. Can you think of any?

84/89	Juliet

---

88   1 3 10 'I have remembered me, . . .'
Lady Capulet may think, rightly, that the Nurse seems to have more influence with Juliet than she does.

24/99	Lady Capulet
86/89	The Nurse

---

89   1 3 18 'Come Lammas Eve at night shall she be fourteen.'
The youth of Romeo and Juliet is important. They are in a world ruled by the old, and they are made as different from them as possible. Unlike the sexual realism of the Nurse and Mercutio, the love between Romeo and Juliet has no possible financial or sordid gain to offer. (What about Paris?) Here the Nurse may be confusing the origin of 'Lammas'–Loaf Mass at harvest festival–with Lamb Mass; hence her ironic pet name for Juliet, whose birthday falls, appropriately, in July.

87/94	Juliet
88/90	The Nurse
66/96	Time

90   1 3 19 'Susan and she–. . .'
Susan, the Nurse's dead child, was 'too good' for her. In what way will Juliet also be 'too good' for the Nurse? Throughout the play the Nurse's generally rambling speech always becomes brief and simple when, as here, it touches upon things for which she truly cares.

59/118	Death and sickness
89/91	The Nurse

91   1 3 23 'That shall she, marry! I remember it well.'
The speech that follows shows the harmless, chatty nature of the Nurse. In conjunction with the barely controlled irritation of Lady Capulet and Juliet it makes a very funny scene, which will temporarily divert the audience from the tragedy to come. The dating of many of Shakespeare's plays is something which always exercises scholars, some of whom have pounced hopefully on the Nurse's mention of an earthquake as perhaps being a topical allusion. No luck–the Nurse's avowedly good memory, and the contents thereof, seem due to a skilful touch of dramatic writing on Shakespeare's part, rather than to real events. There are records of earthquakes in England in 1580, 1583 and 1585, and *Romeo and Juliet* was probably written around the middle of the 1590s.

90/93	The Nurse

92   1 3 31 'When it did taste the wormwood on the nipple . . .'
This is the second reference to drinking in the play. Notice how the association is being made between bitterness and drinking. The imagery of drinking and wine, with its religious and sacramental overtones, is amongst the most complex and subtle in the play.

76/94	The body

93   1 3 40 'And then my husband . . .'
The Nurse is vulgar but not coarse. She has lived through great sadness but looks back on her husband with affection. In her mind a 'merry' husband is of more lasting value than a passionate lover. To her, love is about 'falling backward' with 'a merry man' and having babies. Dramatically, it is interesting that she should mention Juliet in connection with physical love at this point.

85/99	Passion
91/95	The Nurse

94   1 3 45 'The pretty wretch left crying and said "Ay".'
Juliet's 'Ay' stresses the physical side of her nature, as did our being told about her reaction to the wormwood. These hints prepare us for her passionate feelings for Romeo.

89/96	Juliet
92/98	The body

95   1 3 62 'An I might live to see thee married once . . .'
This anticipation of marriage builds up tension in the audience, because they know about Paris's talk with Capulet.

84/101	Aspects of style
93/102	The Nurse

96   1 3 66 'How stands your disposition to be married?'
The abruptness with which Lady Capulet introduces the idea of marriage to
Juliet shows her lack of understanding of a young person's feelings. It
emphasizes the gulf between older people and younger ones—although
Lady Capulet says she is comparatively young, so it also emphasizes the
atmosphere of haste which permeates the play. Juliet's formal reply to her
mother shows both her present childishness and her inexperience of
emotional involvement. Or is she just playing for time? Juliet begins as a
submissive, unawakened girl, but we soon see that courage is her most
outstanding trait as her passions accelerate her into womanhood.

83/121	Age
94/97	Juliet
89/128	Time

97   1 3 67 'It is an honour that I dream not of.'
Juliet will reveal a different side of her nature from this when she has met
Romeo. She will then dream of many things.

0/112	Dreams
96/103	Juliet

98   1 3 69 'I would say thou hadst sucked wisdom from thy teat.'
This is the first of several references to sucking. Notice how Shakespeare
uses this example, and how he uses the others.

94/144	The body

99   1 3 71 'Here in Verona, ladies of esteem . . .'
Lady Capulet gives some insensitive and irrelevant reasons for Juliet to get
married, and this again highlights her lack of understanding about the
situation of young people, even her own daughter.

88/122	Lady Capulet
93/101	Passion

100   1 3 79 'Nay, he's a flower; in faith, a very flower.'
The beauty of youth is again linked with plants—this time rather ironically
with the all-too-brief glory of flowers. Paris's love is of that bookish sort
which Romeo is currently experiencing towards Rosaline. Contrast its
artificiality, as expressed here, with the passion of Romeo's meeting
Juliet—although Romeo is still rather theoretical about matters because Juliet
gently teases him for kissing 'by th' book'. There is a sustained contrast in
the play between the kind of knowledge which is to be found in books, and
the kind which is to be found only in real life. It is the difference between
theory and practice. The Friar, for example, is perhaps a well-meaning and
learned man, but his cunning plans and herbal lore are unable to deal with
the real-life problems of Romeo and Juliet. Notice that Romeo and Juliet both
have flashes of doubt about the wisdom of his counsel.

67/308	Paris
74/148	Plants

101   1 3 82 'Read o'er the volume of young Paris' face, . . .'
Sight and eyes are again associated with love in this rather strained book
image. Notice that Lady Capulet's attitude to marriage is one based upon the
sharing of position and wealth, rather than one based upon the sharing of
love.

95/104	Aspects
	of style
99/102	Passion

102   1 3 96 'No less? Nay, bigger! Women grow by men.'
In contrast to the attitude of Lady Capulet, the Nurse thinks of marriage as
the fulfilment of love, and thinks of all the 'happy nights'.

101/103	Passion
95/138	The Nurse

103   1 3 98 'I'll look to like . . .'
Juliet has promised to 'look to like'. She is almost of a mind to fall in love on
sight—just like Romeo. Interestingly, although Capulet promised her she

81/106	Darkness
	and light

would meet Paris at the banquet, this event never takes place. 'I'll look to like' is in fact nicely ambiguous. Does Juliet mean that she will try to like or that she will like what she sees? If she means the latter, it seems to foreshadow her falling in love on sight with Romeo.

97/123	Juliet
102/108	Passion

104   1 4 4 'We'll have no Cupid hoodwinked with a scarf, . . .'
This is the second reference in the play to the blindfolded Cupid. Here it is linked with puns about party games and the mastering of hawks.

101/105	Aspects of style
48/110	Benvolio

105   1 4 7 'Nor no without-book prologue, . . .'
This is a contemptuous reference, perhaps to an actor who could not read. These lines do not appear in some early versions of the play.

104/112	Aspects of style

106   1 4 11 'Give me a torch.'
Romeo says he will carry the burning torch to light their way, and in so doing makes an ironic comment. It is unfortunately true that he will soon have something to 'bear', and by looking at the way the symbolism of light is used in the play we can work out what it is.

103/111	Darkness and light
80/111	Romeo

107   1 4 13 'Nay, gentle Romeo, . . .'
Mercutio makes his appearance. His wild and fiery nature is appropriate for one with such a name. This mercurial character is volatile and impulsive – his words run away with him in an almost unstoppable, inspired flow. Romeo says of him in Act 2 scene 4, that he 'loves to hear himself talk, and will speak more in a minute than he will stand to in a month'. And at the end of another play, *Love's Labour's Lost*, Shakespeare warns that 'The words of Mercury are harsh'. In mythology Mercury is the swift messenger of Jupiter, the prolific god of love. Mercury itself orbits the sun nearer than any other planet, closest to the fierce heat. Mercutio's notions about love revolve around burning passions, and form a striking contrast to the idealistic love of Romeo. These contrasts in the imagery appear a couple of lines further on, when the references to stillness and to 'a soul of lead' play around Mercutio's entrance into the action.

85/108	Mercutio

108 1 4 17 'You are a lover.'
The notion of romantic love amuses Mercutio. In his subsequent speeches he makes continual and often vulgar reference to making love, rather than to being in love.

107/114	Mercutio
103/136	Passion

109   1 4 19 'I am too sore empiercèd with his shaft . . .'
References to Cupid, arrows, archery and flight can be found in many parts of the play. The extension of this into falconry and the use of hoods, including maidenhood, is also quite frequent. For an interesting cluster of such images, look at Juliet's 'fiery-footed steeds' speech at the start of the second scene of Act 3.

86/114	Creatures

110   1 4 33 'Come, knock and enter; . . .'
In contrast to Mercutio, Benvolio is the practical character who wants to avoid unnecessary trouble, which is in keeping with what we might expect from a character with his name.

104/202	Benvolio

Characters and ideas previous/next comment

111 1 4 38 'I'll be a candle-holder and look on; . . .'
Here the atmosphere is one of mysterious darkness lit only by torches. Romeo is quite content with this at the moment, but soon he will enjoy being dazzled instead.

106/123 Darkness and light
106/117 Romeo

112 1 4 49 'I dreamt a dream tonight.'
The details of Romeo's dream remain a secret. Notice how he has suddenly altered the mood of the scene, just as he did when he made his first entrance in the play.

105/113 Aspects of style
97/114 Dreams

113 1 4 53 'O, then I see Queen Mab hath been with you.'
The rustic folk mythology forms an effective balance to all the other classical references to mythology in the play. Queen Mab appears to be Shakespeare's own invention, or something from local country belief which he introduced into literature.

112/120 Aspects of style

114 1 4 53 'O, then I see Queen Mab hath been with you.'
Mercutio's brilliant imagination sees dreams as wish-fulfilment fantasies. This speech swarms with references to parts of the human body, which increase in repulsiveness as the speech builds to a climax. Look at the contrast between the magical Mab and her coach, and the kind of wishes she releases. Mercutio can see the paradox of the human condition: the beauty to which the human mind can aspire and the mundaneness of most people's ambitions. It is interesting to speculate why Shakespeare decided to give this beautiful poetic speech to such an otherwise bawdy character. Does Mercutio represent the essence of the sheer physical delight of being alive? We can see in him the body and mind at its most extreme intensity, where reality and madness meet in the irrational dreams which stalk the subconscious mind. This speech also has many references to creatures, many of which feature importantly in the play's imagery. For example, it was thought that maggots grew from the fingers of lazy maids. Notice how this particular image connects with the 'worms' imagery in the rest of the play.

109/125 Creatures
112/116 Dreams
108/145 Mercutio
98/115 The body

115 1 4 74 'O'er ladies' lips, who straight on kisses dream, . . .'
The mouth imagery continues to develop towards its final form in the tomb. Here lips are associated with kisses, and then with disease and blisters.

114/121 The body

116 1 4 96 'True. I talk of dreams; . . .'
Mercutio talks of dreams as being 'children of an idle brain' – possibly another one of Shakespeare's quite common references to his own art.

114/166 Dreams

117 1 4 97 'Which are the children of an idle brain, . . .'
Is Mercutio really decrying 'vain fantasy'? He compares dreams with the air 'wooing' the 'frozen bosom of the North' and, getting a cold reception, turning to the warm South. Is this an intentional reference to Romeo and his affections for Rosaline and then for Juliet? If it is, is Mercutio's remark a fair comparison, do you think?

111/118 Romeo
73/119 The elements

	Characters and ideas previous/next comment	

118   1 4 106 'I fear, too early.'
Here Romeo has a premonition of his own death. Interestingly, this premonition is linked with 'this night's revels'. Notice how, near the end of Act 4, another scene of revelry is suddenly changed 'to the contrary', as Capulet puts it.

| 90/139 | Death and sickness |
| 117/119 | Romeo |

119   1 4 112 'But He that hath the steerage of my course . . .'
The sea is often used by Shakespeare as a powerful image of the uncontrollable, unpredictable powers of nature. It is often used, as here, to symbolize fate. In Elizabethan times the uncertainty of the sea made it an effective image for fate, over which man has no control. Who is it who has 'steerage' of Romeo's course through the play? Never mind who Romeo himself has in mind here, as that is fairly obvious, but who is really his pilot? He himself does not seem to know – look at how his attitude has changed by the time he gets to Act 5 scene 3 where, about a third of the way through he calls the poison his 'pilot'.

75/140	Fate
118/125	Romeo
117/160	The elements

120   1 5 1 'Where's Potpan, . . .'
At the end of the last scene the audience was left with a sense of foreboding. The start of this scene, although from the stage directions it would appear to be simply a continuation of the last one, changes the mood to one of everyday domestic concerns. The last words of the servingman, 'and the longer liver take all' is a cheery, if ironical antidote to the atmosphere of death, and makes the next development of the plot more effective in contrast. In many places in the play it is evident that Shakespeare designed the play as one integrated whole, because generally it tends to forge ahead without pause. In any case, Elizabethan scene changes did not usually impede the flow of action.

| 113/124 | Aspects of style |

121   1 5 17 'Welcome gentlemen!'
The whole of Capulet's speech emphasizes the temporary nature of youthful energy. Capulet is too old to dance but enjoys watching the young people. His speech is full of references to physical action and parts of the body, which contrast the hot vigour of youth with the sedateness of age. The play details the joy of life and the short-lived beauty of the body – hence all the references to food, sleep, exercise, love, lust, buds, flowers, the seasons and, of course, death.

| 96/122 | Age |
| 115/126 | The body |

122   1 5 35 'What, man? 'Tis not so much, 'tis not so much.'
Capulet, like many old people, tends to underestimate the time that has passed. Has Lady Capulet done the same in her claim to have been a mother at about fourteen years of age?

| 121/181 | Age |
| 99/130 | Lady Capulet |

123   1 5 44 'O, she doth teach the torches to burn bright!'
Romeo immediately associates Juliet with the brightness of fire, but not with the hot fire of Rosaline. Notice here the first of many references to Juliet's holy qualities.

| 111/132 | Darkness and light |
| 103/124 | Juliet |

124   1 5 47 'Beauty too rich for use, . . .'
Romeo sees Juliet as 'too rich for use, for earth too dear!'. In what way is she 'too dear' for the earth? Consider how the earth will eventually 'use' her at the end of the play.

| 120/133 | Aspects of style |
| 123/134 | Juliet |

	Characters and ideas *previous/next comment*

125 1 5 48 'So shows a snowy dove . . .'
Benvolio's prophecy that Rosaline will look like a crow has come true. Juliet, however, is a 'snowy dove', not a swan.

114/169	Creatures
119/126	Romeo

126   1 5 50 'The measure done, I'll watch her . . .'
The emphasis is still on looking and touching, but this time the touch is a holy one. Romeo has indeed taken Benvolio's earlier advice to 'take some new infection to thy eye'. To what extent will it also prove to be true that 'one pain is lessened by another's anguish'?

125/129	Romeo
79/152	Sight
121/127	The body

127 1 5 54 'This, by his voice, should be a Montague.'
The Elizabethans believed that four 'humours' determined a person's personality – too much of any one of these and they became too bold, too listless, too melancholic or too angry. Which characters in the play represent each of the four humours? Which humour does Tybalt seem to represent, for example?

126/135	The body
22/128	Tybalt

128 1 5 55 'Fetch me my rapier, boy.'
In contrast to Romeo's wondering speech, Tybalt crashes in, as usual spoiling for a fight. This and the previous speech touch upon many of the play's themes.

96/158	Time
127/133	Tybalt

129 1 5 67 'And, to say truth, Verona brags of him . . .'
The only objective comment about Romeo's character comes here. As a 'well-governed youth' presumably he has not been involved in too many fights. It is bad luck that he does get involved later when he least wants to be.

71/130	Lord Capulet
126/134	Romeo

130 1 5 69 'I would not for the wealth of all this town . . .'
Capulet seems quite conscious of the power of money and position. So does Lady Capulet. His anger at Tybalt shows that he has a petulant will hidden under his façade of geniality. This is seen again later in the play, in his dealings with Juliet.

122/236	Lady Capulet
129/131	Lord Capulet

131 1 5 76 'I'll not endure him.'
It is ironic, as well as funny, that Capulet should criticize Tybalt for saying that he will not endure Romeo as a guest at the feast, because Capulet displays exactly this same fiery temperament himself. Capulet will not have Romeo accosted at his feast. Everybody in the play, apart from Tybalt, treats Romeo well – so is there any truth in the suggestion that Romeo is his own worst enemy?

130/272	Lord Capulet

132 1 5 87 'Be quiet, or – More light, more light! – . . .'
Capulet here cries for more light. Later the lovers Romeo and Juliet will call for less, as dawn begins to break. The emphasis on darkness begins to increase in the play.

123/147	Darkness and light

133 1 5 89 'Patience perforce with wilful choler meeting . . .'
Tybalt's comment here prepares us for his next fateful meeting with Romeo. He seems to be just as 'star-crossed' as Romeo. Tybalt's character is revealed

124/135	Aspects of style

	Characters and ideas previous/next comment

both in this speech and in his all-too-true prophecy. How far is Tybalt responsible for the tragedy?

128/231	Tybalt

134   1 5 93 'If I profane with my unworthiest hand . . .'
In this love sonnet which is shared by Romeo and Juliet the overtone is religious, although the emphasis is on the body. Compare this with all the references to paganism in Romeo's speeches about his love for Rosaline. Romeo still uses extravagant, rather forced language when he speaks of Juliet as a 'holy shrine' and himself as a 'pilgrim'.

124/136	Juliet
129/136	Romeo

135   1 5 93 'If I profane with my unworthiest hand . . .'
When taken together, the lines which Romeo and Juliet speak to each other here form a sonnet. This formal use of language gives dignity to their love duet, and adds an almost sacramental quality to the scene. Notice how the imagery of lips and mouths is used here in marked contrast to the way it is used in the rest of the play. Romeo speaks the first quatrain of the sonnet, Juliet the second, and they share the third. Each speaks one line of the closing couplet. They then start another sonnet, with each saying one line of the first quatrain until the fourth, which they share.

133/141	Aspects of style
127/137	The body

136   1 5 103 'O, then, dear saint, let lips do what hands do!'
The lovers' use of language, especially their heavy use of religious words, serves to separate them from the rest of this scene, which bustles with activity. Their exchanges form a kind of duel with words – an interesting link with the action of the rest of the play.

134/137	Juliet
108/138	Passion
134/153	Romeo

137   1 1 110 'You kiss by th' book.'
Juliet gently rebukes Romeo for going too much 'by th' book'. This image was also used earlier by Lady Capulet, of Paris. The two effects are different and worth comparing.

136/139	Juliet
135/142	The body

138   1 5 116 'I tell you, he that can lay hold of her . . .'
This is another interesting association of love with marriage, status with wealth – this time from the Nurse.

136/145	Passion
102/204	The Nurse

139   1 5 135 'My grave is like to be my wedding bed.'
If she cannot marry Romeo she will die. But we know that Juliet is in a worse dilemma than she thinks. This is the first occurrence of the image of death in the guise of a bridegroom. The spiritual love of Romeo and Juliet and the physical kinds of love represented by Mercutio and the Nurse can be connected only through death.

118/150	Death and sickness
137/152	Juliet

140   1 5 138 'My only love, sprung from my only hate!'
Is it possible to separate fate and chance here? If Juliet had known in advance that Romeo was a Montague would it have made any difference?

119/149	Fate

Characters and ideas previous/next comment

141   1 5 138 'My only love, sprung from my only hate!'
The emphasis on opposites returns here with comparisons of enemy and lover, love and hate. It is sometimes difficult to decide whether the play is more about hate than about love, more concerned with death and darkness than with life and light.

135/143   Aspects of style

142   1 5 145 'Anon, anon!'
Many aspects of the body have been introduced so far: the body can be brutal and it can be feeble, it can dance and it can stumble, it can kiss and it can kill. Even its non-physical spiritual attributes have been applauded. Steadily the emphasis of the imagery in the play now turns more and more towards the body's non-physical, spiritual side.

137/144   The body

Act 2

143   2 0 1 'Now old desire doth in his deathbed lie, . . .'
Does this second speech of the Chorus serve any dramatic purpose? There are three sonnets in the play, the Chorus speaks two and the first meeting of Romeo and Juliet produces the third. There are several other different types of poetry in the play – be on the lookout for them, as their use is never accidental.

141/146   Aspects of style

144   2 0 2 'And young affection gapes to be his heir.'
The Chorus echoes the mouth imagery with 'gapes' – meaning to long eagerly, as with an open mouth.

142/156   The body

145   2 1 11 'Speak to my gossip Venus one fair word, . . .'
In this speech Mercutio talks about the pagan deities Venus and Cupid in connection with love, and his references to the body are more to do with lust than love. His subsequent speeches reinforce this physical side of love in the bawdiest way. Mercutio refers to the old story of a King who fell in love with a beggar maid, because of the mischevious intervention of Cupid.

114/146   Mercutio
138/147   Passion

146   2 1 17 'I conjure thee by Rosaline's bright eyes, . . .'
As in his Queen Mab speech, Mercutio appeals to the spirit world in his typically bawdy way.

143/151   Aspects of style
145/193   Mercutio

147   2 1 32 'Blind is his love and best befits the dark.'
Benvolio thinks Romeo is still in love with Rosaline, and associates this unhappy kind of love with darkness.

132/149   Darkness and light
145/148   Passion

148   2 1 34 'Now will he sit under a medlar tree . . .'
Compare Mercutio's coarse fruit imagery with Juliet's association of a rose with Romeo's name. To 'meddle' was bawdy Elizabethan slang. The medlar

147/150   Passion
100/155   Plants

fruit, like a small brown apple, was said to resemble the female sex organs. Why did Shakespeare introduce such a bawdy reference? To understand why, look at the stunning contrast between what is happening in this scene and what happens in the one which follows. Imagine how much more effective still it is when actually performed on stage. Notice how the language and imagery used undergo a sudden lifting of level. Mercutio's erotic extremism is set against Romeo's romantic idealism. The play is full of such contrasts, balances and tensions.

149   2 2 1 'He jests at scars that never felt a wound.'
The connection between the lovers and the idea of being 'star-crossed' is made at once. Notice how many images in this scene are related to this idea. Amid all the bustle and rush of the play only two places are set in stillness – here in the moonlight is one of them. The other is at the end of the play in the tomb. Do we find here the 'artificial night' in which Romeo says he has been living? Romeo's love for Juliet is consistently expressed in terms of light within the darkness. Notice how this particularly effective device is finally developed at the end of the play. What later event in the play is ironically anticipated here in line one? (Hint: think about the words 'scars' and 'wound'. What happens to Mercutio?) This scene division is probably an artificial one in the flow of action. Notice how by having this scene present, the result is that we have to split the couplet shared by Romeo and Benvolio in a rather unfortunate and clumsy way.

147/150	Darkness and light
140/189	Fate

150   2 2 3 'It is the East, and Juliet is the sun!'
Light imagery reaches a climax in this scene of love. Juliet is the source of all light – she is the sun. A few lines later Romeo says that only 'fools', such as Romeo used to be, have anything to do with the 'sick and pale' light of the moon. Romeo connects the pale moonlight with sickness and grief. The moon is characterized as virginal, sick and green. This imagery rises again at the end of the play in Juliet's tomb – here it is used to emphasize the powerful, wholesome and life-giving light which is, metaphorically, Juliet herself. Elizabethan court jesters often wore a costume which was a chequer of 'pale and green' – hence the comment 'none but fools do wear it'.

149/152	Darkness and light
139/159	Death and sickness
148/153	Passion

151   2 2 8 'Her vestal livery is but sick and green, . . .'
'Vestal' means chaste or pure, or related to the Roman goddess Vesta. In ancient Rome the vestal virgins were four (later six) virgin priestesses whose lives were dedicated to Vesta and to maintaining the sacred fire in her temple. Vesta was the Roman goddess of the hearth and of fire.

146/159	Aspects of style

152   2 2 13 'Her eye discourses.'
Eyes have often been called the windows of the soul. Juliet's eyes are not just stars, but the 'fairest stars' in the sky. Romeo expresses the purity of his love, and its highly romantic nature, through imagery full of references to light. Notice the particular quality of light which he concentrates on – very different from that which he used to describe his feelings about Rosaline.

150/159	Darkness and light
139/157	Juliet
126/184	Sight

153 2 2 26 'O, speak again, bright angel!'
Notice that Juliet is not compared to a pagan goddess, like Rosaline was, but

150/154	Passion

to an angel, and to Mercury. Later when Romeo talks about baptism he calls Juliet a saint. These religious references explain the kind of love which Romeo feels for Juliet.

136/158   Romeo

154   2 2 33 'O Romeo, Romeo! – wherefore art thou Romeo?'
The love of Romeo and Juliet is in several ways separated from the rest of the play. For example, this scene sets it physically apart from the action of the rest of the play by using amongst other things the moonlight and the garden. They are also set apart from the feuding and sniping. The love of Romeo and Juliet has a strong sense of the eternal and the pure. Notice how it is the dominant themes from the rest of the play, like the feud and the actions of fate, which now begin to conspire to destroy them and their love.

153/155   Passion

155   2 2 43 'What's in a name?'
Romeo is associated with what always has been regarded by many as the most perfect flower in the garden.

154/156   Passion
148/164   Plants

156   2 2 58 'My ears have not yet drunk a hundred words . . .'
Juliet's reference to her ears drinking in his words emphasizes the idea that all her senses are awakened. Sight is also involved through the reference to the written word of books. Shakespeare used this idea in another context in the play *Hamlet*, where the hero's sleeping father is murdered by poison being poured into his ear. Some of this feeling creeps into Juliet's use of the drinking-of-words image later in the play.

155/157   Passion
144/170   The body

157   2 2 62 'How camest thou hither, tell me, . . .'
Though in love, and very young, Juliet keeps her head. This and her next few utterances show that she has a strong will.

152/161   Juliet
156/160   Passion

158   2 2 67 'For stony limits cannot hold love out, . . .'
The importance of haste is now an idea which is taken up by Romeo. What do you think are the other 'stony limits' which will later also fail to keep out Romeo? (Hint: this is an anticipation of a place found at the end of the play.) The 'stony limits' of the tomb 'cannot hold love out' in more ways than one. Notice how Romeo's comments prepare the audience for Juliet's desperate measures later, by mentioning the way love dares to attempt anything which can be done.

153/166   Romeo
128/163   Time

159   2 2 77 'My life were better ended by their hate . . .'
Romeo unwittingly foretells his own death here, surrounded by the imagery of darkness. In this play Shakespeare frequently introduces such omens of death. Romeo says he would rather have his life ended quickly by being discovered by Juliet's kinsmen, 'ended by their hate' as he puts it, than die suffering slowly without the love of Juliet. Ironically, this is the way things finally turn out.

151/162   Aspects of style
152/162   Darkness and light
150/167   Death and sickness

160   2 2 82 'I am no pilot; . . .'
This would have been a very meaningful image to the Elizabethan audience. The sea was *the* great challenge to the Elizabethans, offering untold riches if

157/161   Passion
119/165   The elements

*Characters and ideas
previous/next comment*

it could be conquered. Notice how the image of the pilot has occured again, this time as Romeo talks about the sea; the symbol of the great unpredictable forces of fate.

161   2 2 88 'Fain would I dwell on form − . . .'
Juliet's honesty is not merely the honesty of a child, as she shows at line 92. If he wants her to flirt she will, but it goes against her character. Juliet says the gods laugh at lovers' promises, because they are often wrapped up in deceitful language. She urges Romeo to speak honestly of his feelings. Often in Shakespeare's plays we find elaborate language equated with falseness and lies. Plain speaking, without the use of fanciful, 'intellectual' references, is often equated in Shakespeare's work with the telling of the truth.

157/163	Juliet
160/162	Passion

162   2 2 109 'O, swear not by the moon, th' inconstant moon, . . .'
Romeo often used the imagery of light to describe his love for Rosaline, and now does so for Juliet. Here he wants to swear by the light of the moon (a pagan deity), but Juliet says the moon's light is not constant. Juliet has no time for flowery talk, and Romeo's speeches in the play become steadily less artificial and love-sick after he meets Juliet.

159/167	Aspects of style
159/168	Darkness and light
161/164	Passion

163   2 2 118 'It is too rash, too unadvised, too sudden; . . .'
Juliet fears this haste as much as Romeo revels in it. She is afraid of being 'quickly won'. The imagery she uses is very expressive and powerful. How accurate is her vision of their love as lightning in a storm? This storm is also an image for the storm of conflict, parental rage and death in the rest of the play.

161/167	Juliet
158/183	Time

164   2 2 121 'This bud of love, . . .'
Juliet says that the bud of love should grow naturally into a flower. What do references to growth suggest about the nature of their love? What do they prepare us for as a natural development?

162/165	Passion
155/176	Plants

165   2 2 133 'My bounty is as boundless as the sea, . . .'
The lovers are tightly identified with the almost mystical powers of nature, like the sea and the sky. Consider the effect that this creates.

164/168	Passion
160/207	The elements

166   2 2 139 'O blessèd, blessèd night! I am afeard, . . .'
A dream-like atmosphere has haunted the play since Mercutio's 'Queen Mab' speech. The image of sweetness has also arisen several times, and between Mercutio's speech and its final development it is always associated with the same thing in the play − what is it? In its final form we see it in the tomb, where Romeo says to Juliet that death 'hath sucked the honey of thy breath'. Juliet shows herself to be an eminently practical person who begins making plans, unlike Romeo, who lives only for the moment − notice his reaction here as soon as she leaves for example.

116/324	Dreams
158/174	Romeo

167   2 2 149 'Madam!'
This calling of Juliet by the Nurse is a pre-echo of that in the fifth scene of Act 4.

162/169	Aspects of style
163/170	Juliet
159/172	Death and sickness

168 2 2 155 'A thousand times the worse, to want thy light!'
Romeo now associates Juliet with the light of day. Night therefore cannot be good. The clever schoolboy image speaks for itself!

162/173	Darkness and light
165/182	Passion

---

169 2 2 158 'Hist! Romeo, hist!'
Juliet here imagines Romeo as a hunting falcon and he thinks of her as a young nestling. Almost 20 lines later she sees him as a tame bird on a silken thread which she holds. The way they see each other is revealed in the imagery, but notice how other hints are dropped by the imagery also, for instance about the way their love takes flight in the first place, how Romeo has to flee, the speed with which the action of the play proceeds, and so on.

167/170	Aspects of style
125/171	Creatures

---

170 2 2 160 'Bondage is hoarse and may not speak aloud, . . .'
The imagery of the mouth and of calling is extended to Echo, the broken-hearted Greek nymph of caverns who repeated what was spoken to her. How prophetic is the picture which Juliet draws with her imagery here?

169/172	Aspects of style
167/171	Juliet
156/177	The body

---

171 2 2 176 ''Tis almost morning. I would have thee gone.'
Juliet uses many references to birds and to falconry, which is very appropriate because swiftness and flight will soon become important in the action of the play.

169/194	Creatures
170/185	Juliet

---

172 2 2 183 'Yet I should kill thee with much cherishing.'
How does Juliet kill Romeo by loving him?

170/173	Aspects of style
167/182	Death and sickness

---

173 2 2 188 'The grey-eyed morn smiles on the frowning night, . . .'
As the scene began, so is it beautifully rounded off, with light chasing away the darkness. The merging of the imagery of light, night and the face makes the ending a perfect mirror for the way the scene began. Many such symmetries exist in the play.

172/174	Aspects of style
168/211	Darkness and light

---

174 2 2 190 'And darkness fleckled like a drunkard reels . . .'
The Titans were the first gods in Greek mythology – Hyperion was father of the sun, moon and dawn, and drove a chariot across the sky. From the point of view of the play's construction, notice how skilfully this anticipates Juliet's 'gallop apace' speech and prepares also for the entry of the Friar.

173/175	Aspects of style
166/182	Romeo

---

175 2 3 1 'Now, ere the sun advance his burning eye . . .'
The Friar speaks consistently in rhyme, which helps to set him quietly apart from the bustle of the rest of the play, where rhyme is not used in this concentrated form. Shakespeare wanted us to sense that the Friar was different from other characters. What kind of function does the Friar fulfil in the play?

174/176	Aspects of style

176   2 3 1 'Now, ere the sun advance his burning eye . . .'
After the intense emotion of the previous scene, think about the dramatic purpose of this reflective speech. The prolonged garden metaphor mentions two opposing qualities in plants and people: some plants contain reviving medicine as well as poison and people also are likewise a mixture of good and evil. This important idea in the play appears in many guises – for example: love and hate, life and death, passion and reason, light and dark.

175/179	Aspects of style	
164/209	Plants	
0/178	The Friar	

177   2 3 7 'And from her womb . . .'
This is the second reference to sucking – the first was from the Nurse in the third scene of Act 1. How is this imagery used? Amongst other things it is being associated with the idea of nourishment, the drawing of food, goodness and wisdom from the 'earthy' characters and characteristics mentioned in the play. The mouth imagery is closely bound up with the ideas of Nature; the earth is depicted as a nourisher and reclaimer of its own children. The Nurse represents a kind of large and bawdy 'Earth-mother' for Juliet. The Friar is closely connected with the herbal lore and the mystical relationship between the plant world of nature and man. It is in this setting that Death as Juliet's ravisher stalks the play, almost as a character in its own right.

170/182   The body

178   2 3 17 'Virtue itself turns vice, being misapplied, . . .'
The Friar can be seen to represent the Protestant Elizabethans' view of the scheming Catholic Church, always meddling, and whose own 'virtue' has turned to 'vice, being misapplied'. How far is the Friar's comment applicable to his own actions in helping Romeo and Juliet?

176/179   The Friar

179   2 3 25 'And where the worser is predominant, . . .'
This speech is in some ways a parallel to Mercutio's 'Queen Mab' speech. Both put forward interpretations of what is real in the world. Both see maturity, when it has gone astray, as 'canker'. How does all this relate to what is going on in the rest of the play? The different aspects of human nature which the speeches mention are often to be found represented in the characters in the play. For example, here the Friar talks about 'rude will' and how it is self-destructive, which might well describe Tybalt.

176/188	Aspects of style	
178/180	The Friar	

180   2 3 26 'Full soon the canker death . . .'
When evil predominates in man then sickness and death will follow. The Friar seems to be a man of simple interests and philosophy. The Friar's character serves as a useful contrast to the aggressive and fiery atmosphere of much of the rest of the play.

179/184   The Friar

181   2 3 31 'Care keeps his watch in every old man's eye, . . .'
What could highlight the old people's misunderstanding of young people better than the suggestion that young people have no worries!

122/211   Age

182   2 3 45 'I have been feasting with mine enemy, . . .'
Romeo's image of love as a wound which the Friar can heal is ironic, because the Friar's 'physic' for Juliet has disastrous consequences. Romeo's speech combines the imagery of food, love-sickness and medicine. This imagery sums up much of Romeo's own personal development in the play so far.

172/192	Death and sickness	
168/183	Passion	
174/186	Romeo	
177/199	The body	

Characters and ideas previous/next comment

183   2 3 57 'By holy marriage.'
Notice how the jerky sound of these two lines gives the impression of breathless speed, which mirrors the speed with which Romeo and Juliet have fallen in love.

182/186	Passion
163/190	Time

184   2 3 63 'So soon forsaken?'
The Friar's observation at this point is very appropriate, but think carefully about the use of the imagery of looking and seeing in the play. The Friar's remark is true at a deep level, and it raises questions about the love of Romeo and Juliet.

152/229	Sight
180/185	The Friar

185   2 3 76 'Women may fall when there's no strength in men.'
This remark by the Friar is an interesting contrast to Sampson's jests in Act 1. How true is it in Juliet's case?

171/210	Juliet
184/186	The Friar

186   2 3 78 'For doting, not for loving, pupil mine.'
The Friar saw clearly that Romeo's feeling for Rosaline was infatuation.

183/195	Passion
182/187	Romeo
185/187	The Friar

187   2 3 80 'To lay one in, another out to have.'
This comment by the Friar has an ominous ring to it. Also it points up the parallels in the play between the worlds of life, death and twilight. In addition it is dramatically ironic, because we know how the story ends.

186/195	Romeo
186/188	The Friar

188   2 3 84 'Thy love did read by rote, that could not spell.'
The reading/writing metaphor perfectly reflects the idea of Romeo going through the motions of love without understanding what love was. Several characters in the play seem to notice Romeo's tendency to use the ornate and flowery language of conventional love poetry.

179/192	Aspects of style
187/189	The Friar

189   2 3 87 'For this alliance may so happy prove . . .'
The Friar is optimistic and seems unaware of the complexity of human relationships and the pitfalls of fate. In fairness to the Friar however, he may be right after all. Were it not for the servants, who fight because they always have done, we can see that the feud is a quarrel which is ready for settling. The Friar is perhaps right to think that a marriage may do the trick.

149/191	Fate
188/190	The Friar

190   2 3 89 'O, let us hence! I stand on sudden haste.'
This line seems to sum up Romeo's nature and explain one cause of his downfall. But what weaknesses of the Friar, as revealed around line 90, indirectly contribute to the tragedy?

189/216	The Friar
183/193	Time

191   2 4 6 'Tybalt, the kinsman to old Capulet, . . .'
Shakespeare never lets the audience escape for long from the sense of doom which hovers in the background throughout the play.

189/218	Fate

192   2 4 13 'Alas, poor Romeo, he is already dead!'
Mercutio suggests that Romeo is as good as dead through love, and in no position to fight with Tybalt. Ironically this is true, although not in the way Mercutio seems to have in mind.

188/196   Aspects of style
182/200   Death and sickness

193   2 4 28 'The pox of such antic, lisping . . .'
In this speech Mercutio ridicules the new fashion for the Italian style of fencing with the rapier which was much scorned in England at this time on account of its precise, almost dance-like technique. The implication here is that such fencing is too much 'by th' book', to quote Juliet's comment about Romeo's kissing. The suggestion is that ornate speech or mannered behaviour is fundamentally false and affected. When seen in this light, Romeo's entrance at this point almost becomes a criticism of him. Does his ridicule extend, by implication, to anything else in the play?

146/194   Mercutio
190/210   Time

194   2 4 37 'Without his roe, like a dried herring.'
Mercutio takes up the bawdy imagery of fish which was introduced at the start of the play. Such images often run throughout a particular Shakespeare play, and form a kind of underlying skeleton to the language, relating the dramatic action to the characters.

171/232   Creatures
193/198   Mercutio

195   2 4 39 '. . . that Petrarch flowed in. Laura, to his lady . . .'
Mercutio is wittily drawing attention to the fact that Petrarch's form of the sonnet is the one used in the play. Petrarch wrote rather tearfully of his love for Laura de Noves in a way which was copied throughout Europe and whose style came to be known as the 'Petrarchan Sonnet'. This style is noticeable in Romeo's love speeches.

186/197   Passion
187/197   Romeo

196 2 4 41 '–Dido a dowdy, Cleopatra a gypsy, . . .'
Mercutio's speech at this point is full of references to mythology. These might be rather obscure for students today, because of the differences between 16th-century English schooling and ours. Tales from classical literature and the Bible were far more widely known then than is the case now.

192/198   Aspects of style

197   2 4 55 'A most courteous exposition.'
Compare the way Romeo can share a joke with Mercutio now that he is genuinely in love, with his misery when he thought he was in love with Rosaline.

195/200   Passion
195/201   Romeo

198   2 4 66 'Come between us, good Benvolio!'
Mercutio's invitation to 'come between us' is ironic. It is Romeo's love for his friend which produces disaster, as he comes between Tybalt and Mercutio. The idea that love leads to disaster is an ironic omen.

196/201   Aspects of style
194/201   Mercutio

199   2 4 78 'Thy wit is a very bitter sweeting.'
This is one of several references in the play to fruit, especially apples. Here the image is appropriately used to describe Romeo's sharp wit.

182/208   The body

200   2 4 86 'Why, is not this better now than groaning . . .'
Romeo's real love for Juliet has cured the sickness of his love for Rosaline, although Mercutio does not realize this.

Characters and ideas	
previous/next comment	
192/219	Death and sickness
197/208	Passion

201 2 4 91 'Stop there, stop there!'
This verbal duelling between Romeo and Mercutio prepares us for another kind of duelling, although the emphasis here is on comedy. By emphasizing the comic elements at this point, the play is building towards the sudden change of atmosphere in the next scene.

198/203	Aspects of style
198/202	Mercutio
197/203	Romeo

202   2 4 109 ''Tis no less, I tell ye.'
Benvolio has previously warned Mercutio that his bawdiness is becoming too extreme, but Mercutio cannot resist twisting even the most commonplace remark to another meaning.

110/227	Benvolio
201/204	Mercutio

203   2 4 112 'One, gentlewoman, that God hath made . . .'
This comment of Romeo's may only be a joke, but it will be proved sadly true. What is it about Mercutio's character that will cause him to 'mar' himself?

201/205	Aspects of style
201/206	Romeo

204   2 4 144 'A gentleman, Nurse, that loves to hear . . .'
What have Mercutio and the Nurse got in common? Mercutio dominated the first half of this scene with Romeo just as the Nurse dominates the second. Romeo's comment at this point follows upon Mercutio's exit, but it is a comment which is true of both Mercutio and the Nurse.

202/213	Mercutio
138/212	The Nurse

205   2 4 177 'Some means to come to shrift this afternoon, . . .'
Note the change here from prose to poetry when Romeo begins to talk of Juliet.

203/206	Aspects of style

206   2 4 183 'And stay, good Nurse, behind the abbey wall.'
Apart from what Romeo says about Juliet, both here and a few lines back and both in blank verse, all the rest of this scene is in prose. Think about Shakespeare's use of language and consider why blank verse is more appropriate here.

205/207	Aspects of style
203/207	Romeo

207   2 4 185 'And bring thee cords made like a tackled stair, . . .'
The sea and ships were of great interest in Shakespeare's London, so it is not surprising that they are used in his imagery. The Nurse's flowing gown on her ample body has already been compared to a sail in a full breeze. The next three lines sustain the metaphor of sailing ships.

206/210	Aspects of style
206/219	Romeo
165/234	The elements

208   2 4 196 'Lord! when 'twas a little prating thing—. . .'
In Elizabethan England it was customary for a diner to bring his own knife to the table. It is significant that the Nurse sees Paris's love as being on this material level.

200/211	Passion
199/217	The body

209 2 4 202 'Doth not rosemary and Romeo begin both with a letter?'
The Nurse here associates rosemary with Romeo; Juliet is fond of both she says. In the middle of his first long speech after the discovery of Juliet's body by the Nurse, the Friar also mentions rosemary, this time in connection with Juliet. What he has to say gives the present reference a ring of doom, for rosemary is traditionally the flower of remembrance. Later in the play the Nurse casts rosemary on the body of Juliet.

176/262	Plants

210 2 5 1 'The clock struck nine . . .'
Juliet is now infected with the urge for speed, she says love's messengers should travel as fast as the sun flickers when the clouds blow over it. This is an unusual and interesting connection between the theme of haste and the imagery of light. We have already seen how the imagery of light can be used to express swiftness, when Juliet comments to Romeo that some kinds of love are over as quickly as lightning strikes. This example reinforces this connection.

207/211	Aspects of style
185/212	Juliet
193/220	Time

211 2 5 4 'O, she is lame!'
The imagery of light, the sun and shining stars has already been much used on one occasion in the play. The imagery appears again here, to rise to a climax at the start of the second scene in Act 3. Shakespeare frequently used the imagery in his plays in this way – that is as a sort of skeleton upon which to build the action. The imagery, although it changes and grows as the play progresses, also helps join all of the parts of the play together into one seamless flow of action. This whole scene is about the contrast between the impatience of youth and the slowness of age; the blood rushes to Juliet's cheeks, but the Nurse has an aching head and back.

181/221	Age
210/214	Aspects of style
173/214	Darkness and light
208/215	Passion

212 2 5 21 'Now, good sweet Nurse – . . .'
This conversation between Juliet and the Nurse makes an interesting comparison with that which took place between Romeo and the Friar in scene three of this Act. Both conversations show youth contrasted with age. The Friar's attitude makes him appear wise and kindly. How would you describe the Nurse's attitude?

210/225	Juliet
204/213	The Nurse

213 2 5 38 'Well, you have made a simple choice.'
The Nurse's summary of Romeo is full of physical description and parallels Mercutio's earlier description of Rosaline. This tells us more about the similarities between the characters of the Nurse and Mercutio.

204/227	Mercutio
212/215	The Nurse

214 2 5 62 'Are you so hot?'
This reference by the Nurse to Juliet's 'heat' reappears again a few lines further on, where it is connected to passion and blood. Notice how the first scene of the next Act also begins in heat and ends in blood.

211/216	Aspects of style
211/222	Darkness and light

215 2 5 76 'But you shall bear the burden soon . . .'
Again we see how the Nurse's attitude to love emphasizes the pleasures of sex as being very important.

211/236	Passion
213/270	The Nurse

		Characters and ideas previous/next comment

216   2 6 1 'So smile the heavens . . .'
This short scene prefaces the marriage of Romeo and Juliet, although the Friar's opening words to Romeo might seem ironic to the audience. His remarks at the start of his second speech here might seem more fitting, or prophetic.

214/220   Aspects of style
190/220   The Friar

217   2 6 1 'So smile the heavens . . .'
The mouth imagery is rather chilling here. The Friar talks about the marriage of Romeo and Juliet, and says the Heavens will 'smile' on it – but a few lines further on Romeo calls death 'love-devouring'. Who do you think is correct?

208/223   The body

218   2 6 3 'Amen, amen!'
The atmosphere of doom lies heavy on this scene, in which many of the play's themes can clearly be seen. How many can you detect? Check the 'Summaries of themes' section to help you see how many of them are at work here.

191/230   Fate

219   2 6 7 'Then love-devouring death . . .'
Tempting fate is always risky – here especially so because Romeo is taunting death. He says he will defy death even if it means that he can have only one minute with Juliet. Sadly, fate will allow him very little more than this.

200/233   Death and sickness
207/225   Romeo

220   2 6 9 'These violent delights have violent ends . . .'
One of the central suggestions of the play is that the excess of any passion will lead to tragedy and that passion must therefore be tempered by reason. The Friar's speech here is a small lecture on this point. Why then does he agree to help the lovers in their dangerous conspiracy? He even suggests the plan of action! The Friar is also being used to reflect the fears Juliet expressed in the balcony scene: 'it is too rash . . . too like the lightning'.

216/226   Aspects of style
216/223   The Friar
210/222   Time

221   2 6 9 'These violent delights have violent ends . . .'
Age is depicted here as wise but sad; youth as eager and swift. This quiet scene, which comes just before the explosion in the story, is almost exactly halfway through the play.

211/264   Age

222   2 6 9 'These violent delights have violent ends . . .'
Images of lightning and explosion occur throughout the play. They are particularly appropriate when applied to the love of Romeo and Juliet, as here in this comment by the Friar.

214/243   Darkness and light
220/224   Time

223   2 6 11 'Which as they kiss consume. The sweetest honey . . .'
The Friar's innocent reference here to honey is taken up again by Romeo when, in the tomb, he speaks of death as a bee which 'sucked the honey' of Juliet's breath.

217/250   The body
220/224   The Friar

224   2 6 15 'Too swift arrives as tardy as too slow.'
The Friar's remark here will prove to be true on two separate occasions at the end of the play. Can you think which two places these are?

223/259   The Friar
222/239   Time

225   2 6 18 'A lover may bestride the gossamers . . .'
Romeo comments on Juliet's happiness; we might translate it as 'she walks on air'. His summery images create a peaceful atmosphere which is shattered by the next scene.

212/241	Juliet
219/230	Romeo

Act 3

226   3 1 1 'I pray thee, good Mercutio, . . .'
Unusually for Shakespeare, there is no sub-plot in this play of extreme contrasts. The simple and clear design tends to give the play a relentless feeling. From this point onwards the story requires that the dramatic importance of Romeo increases. From the playwright's point of view this means that Mercutio's current prominence in the action of the play must be decreased; he has, after all, held much of the audience's attention so far.

220/227	Aspects of style

227   3 1 1 'I pray thee, good Mercutio, . . .'
As usual the prudent Benvolio is all for caution. The events of the plot have started to move very quickly; this short conversation between Benvolio and Mercutio halts the pace only momentarily, whilst increasing the suspense. This scene is a turning point in the play, hence the quite appropriate references to heat and passion.

226/228	Aspects of style
202/237	Benvolio
213/228	Mercutio

228   3 1 5 'Thou art like one of these fellows that, . . .'
How ironic are Mercutio's remarks here? Is he really talking about someone other than Benvolio? Mercutio's comment 10 lines further on is obviously not true. Who is he really describing?

227/233	Aspects of style
227/229	Mercutio

229   3 1 53 'Men's eyes were made to look, . . .'
Much of the imagery of eyes is to do with loving looks. The different use of the image here is because this is more appropriate to Mercutio's character.

228/231	Mercutio
184/296	Sight

230   3 1 55 'Well, peace be with you, sir.'
If only Romeo had not gone to look for Benvolio and Mercutio, the situation might have been saved; or would it? Line 61 is the moment for which the action of the play has been preparing us. We know what is in the balance when Romeo answers here. The meaning of Romeo's answer is plain only to us – it is the old riddling Romeo who answers, but how he has changed! Notice that Shakespeare uses the quarrel, and Mercutio's death, to produce a change in Romeo. It is this change, not really anything external, that determines the main tragedy. Within one hundred words Shakespeare brings his hero from the heights to the depths.

218/235	Fate
225/234	Romeo

231   3 1 72 'O calm, dishonourable, vile submission!'
If only Romeo had confided in his friends about his love for Tybalt's kinswoman Juliet, this misunderstanding would not have arisen. It probably would not, however, have made any difference to Tybalt's behaviour. Both Mercutio and Tybalt fight because of what they are. Both have inherently excitable natures and in their death two extremes have met. The symmetry of this pattern is repeated later in the play. (Hint: next time it involves two themes, not two characters.)

229/233	Mercutio
133/232	Tybalt

232   3 1 74 'Tybalt, you ratcatcher, will you walk?'
Mercutio adds a further insulting slant to his previous reference to the 'prince of cats'. Tybalt, from whose name we get 'tibby', has now become a ratcatcher. In the same vein, Mercutio calls his fatal wound a scratch. What was 'low', in the sense of a low animal, about the way Tybalt wounded Mercutio? Compare this action with the way Mercutio bravely accepts death.

194/246	Creatures
231/0	Tybalt

233   3 1 116 'O Romeo, Romeo, brave Mercutio is dead!'
Mercutio and the Nurse rival Romeo and Juliet as leading characters in the early part of the play. Mercutio's death and the Nurse's betrayal of Juliet's trust both solve this problem of emphasis from the dramatist's point of view and simultaneously provide further drive for the action of the play. After Mercutio's death events move very rapidly. In only one scene before the end of the play do we find neither Rome nor Juliet on stage, and there is never any real relaxing of tension or speed from now on. Mercutio was not afraid to die, but there is a double meaning in the idea that he scorned the earth; he made continual fun of everything and everybody on earth, and he scorned the power of fate.

228/237	Aspects of style
219/240	Death and sickness
231/0	Mercutio

234   3 1 124 'And fire-eyed fury be my conduct now!'
The natural elements are seen as being neutral in the affairs of men. Here fire is associated with anger, in the same way as it will be linked with the light of the sun at the beginning of the next scene. Do the characters in the play always see the forces of nature as being neutral in their affairs? Would the Friar see it this way? Would Romeo or Mercutio?

230/235	Romeo
207/252	The elements

235   3 1 136 'O, I am fortune's fool!'
Romeo sees himself as the plaything of chance; he recognizes the trap that fate has caught him in. But how far are his own character and the mistakes he has made really to blame for the situation?

230/259	Fate
234/253	Romeo

236   3 1 149 'For blood of ours shed blood of Montague.'
The violent theme of the feud is taken up by Lady Capulet. Her reactions seem to be as one-dimensional as those of Tybalt. Think about whether her character ever changes or develops during the play. Do some of the other characters develop?

130/238	Lady Capulet
215/238	Passion

237   3 1 152 'Tybalt, here slain, . . .'
Once again Benvolio is used to render a faithful account. With this speech he vanishes from the play. What part has he played in the plot and why is he not needed any more? At this critical turning point in the action of the play, we see Benvolio being used rather like the Chorus to clarify matters. Compare Shakespeare's use of this dramatic device with a similar one at the Prince's next entrance. Benvolio's disappearance is a good example of Shakespeare the dramatist at work. Benvolio was a contrast to two other characters (which ones?) and now he is no longer needed.

233/240	Aspects of style
227/0	Benvolio

238   3 1 181 'Romeo slew Tybalt. Romeo must not live.'
Lady Capulet seems to be a very limited woman, intellectually. She hangs on to a single idea grimly, and as a result rather overdoes her argument. She is a good example of how single-mindedness and anger can prevent people from being civilized and tolerant. This is an important idea in the play, with

236/286	Lady Capulet
236/245	Passion

significant implications for the main characters. Read the character outlines on page 71 and use these to study to what extent different characters allow blindness and passion to destroy their lives.

---

239   3 1 187 'Immediately we do exile him hence.'
Unrestrained passion has rapidly resulted in two deaths and a banishment. This acceleration in the action is further increased in the next scene and makes the sense of urgency in the play more apparent.

224/241	Time

---

240   3 1 192 'I will be deaf to pleading and excuses.'
Who else will be similarly 'deaf' to pleading later on in the play? What parallel is here being subtly drawn between the two situations? Compare the situation at this point in the action with that where Juliet and her father exchange words near the end of scene 5 in Act 3. The Prince's philosophical remark about mercy has a rather threatening sound. Shakespeare ends the scene on an ominous note, ringing with irony. Romeo will still die, even though he has been pardoned.

237/241	Aspects of style
233/244	Death and sickness

---

241   3 2 1 'Gallop apace, you fiery-footed steeds, . . .'
So far in this Act we have seen heated street violence, a climax in the action culminating in deaths, and the quiet solemn Prince. And now we return to Juliet. The increase in the pace of action serves to compress the sense of time. In the lovers' private universe events will also take place in accelerated time. The play begins to move even faster and events 'gallop'. We might expect the language which is used to complement the events taking place. This would lead us to expect short, abrupt exchanges between the characters, heavily punctuated, split into short phrases, like this sentence. But Juliet always speaks in poetry, and Shakespeare has given her the most beautiful of the poetry. Is this an example of the playwright's poor use of language? Or do you think that Shakespeare had in mind a more important priority?

240/242	Aspects of style
225/242	Juliet
239/242	Time

---

242   3 2 1 'Gallop apace, you fiery-footed steeds, . . .'
Juliet's repeated emphasis on Phaëton and night is reminiscent of the play's references to blinded Cupid, fate and death. In mythology, Phaëton almost destroyed the Universe when he recklessly drove the Sun's fiery chariot past Earth. The sense of the urgent passing of time is overpowering throughout the play.

241/245	Aspects of style
241/243	Juliet
241/271	Time

---

243   3 2 5 'Spread thy close curtain, love-performing night, . . .'
The darkness here is not associated with unhappiness but with the secrecy which the lovers are forced to observe.

222/247	Darkness and light
242/244	Juliet

---

244   3 2 10 'It best agrees with night. Come, civil night, . . .'
Swimming just under the surface of the imagery here is the recurring idea in the play that Death, in the form of a lover, is coming to claim Juliet's maidenhead in the darkness.

240/251	Death and sickness
243/245	Juliet

---

245   3 2 13 'Played for a pair of stainless maidenhoods.'
Although in this comment Juliet is thinking of love's fulfilment, the emphasis is also on her and Romeo's virginal innocence. Compare the effect

242/249	Aspects of style

	Characters and ideas previous/next comment	

here with the lovers' last meeting. Notice how closely packed are the opposites in the imagery. This use of opposites (oxymoron) is designed to achieve a particular effect; can you see what it is? (Hint: consider Juliet's state of mind. How can the dramatist make the audience aware of this?)

244/247	Juliet	
238/246	Passion	

246   3 2 17 'Come, night. Come, Romeo.'

It is night-time, but Juliet says that Romeo makes it day. His white body at night will be like snow on a raven.

232/254	Creatures
245/256	Passion

247   3 2 21 'Give me my Romeo. And when I shall die, . . .'

Romeo's brightness makes the night brighter than day. The star imagery echoes that used in Romeo's first speech in the balcony scene. Notice the way death is part of Juliet's imagery. What particular quality of light and darkness is being valued here?

243/269	Darkness and light
245/248	Juliet

248   3 2 30 'To an impatient child . . .'

This skilful touch by Shakespeare cleverly emphasizes both Juliet's youth and her desire for haste. The fact that Juliet is young deepens the joy of her love, and our sorrow at the final tragedy.

247/250	Juliet
242/271	Time

249   3 2 39 'Can heaven be so envious?'

The suggestion here is that the love between Romeo and Juliet is so pure that it will tempt the gods to become envious. How accurate is this guess of Juliet's? The extended punning on the words 'I' and 'Ay' (around line 43) is typical of Shakespeare's dramas.

245/255	Aspects of style

250   3 2 59 'Vile earth, to earth resign; . . .'

This is a prophetic comment. A loose translation might be 'ashes to ashes, dust to dust'. Her passion will indeed lead her to 'resign' herself to death.

248/251	Juliet
223/266	The body

251   3 2 60 'And thou and Romeo press one heavy bier!'

Although we can see how Juliet has misunderstood the Nurse (who was talking about Tybalt, not Romeo), her comment is still very ironic.

244/258	Death and sickness
250/253	Juliet

252   3 2 64 'What storm is this that blows so contrary?'

The confusion of the Nurse's speech is appropriately reflected in Juliet's image of a gusting storm. But the question, 'What storm is this that blows so contrary?' is one of the central issues raised by the whole play. How you answer the question depends on what you decide that the imagery of the storm relates most to: the relationships between people, the civil disorder which the Prince is so concerned about, or the world of dreams, hate, or love.

234/254	The elements

253   3 2 68 'For who is living, if those two are gone?'

Although this question of Juliet's concerns Romeo and Tybalt, it also prepares us for the situation at the end of the play. In *Romeo and Juliet*, the two main characters between them represent many of the joys and passions of life – intense and lived to the full and seen through the eyes of vigorous youth. The world of young people is decimated by the end of the play and in that sense much that was 'living' has indeed 'gŏne' from the world of the

251/255	Juliet
235/260	Romeo

Montagues and Capulets. But does the play actually provide any answer to Juliet's difficult question?

---

254   3 2 73 'O serpent heart, hid with a flowering face!'
Compare this speech with that of Romeo in the first scene of the play ('bright smoke, cold fire'). In what way is Juliet's state of mind similar to Romeo's then? Notice the use of creatures, such as the serpent, raven and wolf, to suggest dark and dangerous qualities.

The use of oxymoron (opposites) here concentrates many references found scattered throughout the rest of the play. The overall effect is to compare Romeo with death. Death as the figure of Juliet's lover is a chilling idea which grows larger, rising nearer the surface of the imagery, as the play moves towards the tomb scene.

246/261	Creatures
252/291	The elements

---

255   3 2 83 'Was ever book containing such vile matter . . .'
Compare this echo with Lady Capulet's description of Paris in the first Act.

249/266	Aspects of style
253/256	Juliet

---

256   3 2 90 'Blistered be thy tongue . . .'
Juliet's anger at the Nurse's remark shows her loyalty to Romeo. She quickly recovers from her initial reaction to the news of the death of Tybalt.

255/258	Juliet
246/257	Passion

---

257 3 2 122 'Romeo is banishèd' – to speak that word . . .'
Juliet's reaction here to Romeo's banishment makes an interesting comparison to Romeo's own view of it – which we do not learn until the next scene. They both feel that to separate them is to condemn them to death – Juliet even says that death will take her 'maidenhead'.

256/263	Passion

---

258   3 2 124 'All slain, all dead.'
Throughout this and Juliet's next speech the idea is emphasized that she and Romeo are already dead. How true is it that in a sense their fate was sealed from the moment they met? They are called 'star-crossed'; notice how many meanings there are to this, depending on whether you interpret it to be a good or a bad thing.

251/282	Death and sickness
256/280	Juliet

---

259   3 3 2 'Affliction is enamoured of thy parts, . . .'
The Friar tells Romeo that his fate is not death but banishment. The audience know that eventually this will in fact be reversed. Ironically the Friar echoes the imagery of the death-lover which we have just heard from Juliet, when she talked about being 'wedded to calamity'.

235/260	Fate
224/267	The Friar

---

260   3 3 17 'There is no world without Verona walls, . . .'
If Romeo had not met Juliet, this banishment would not have been so terrible for him. Fate is turning the knife in the wound.

259/279	Fate
253/261	Romeo

---

261   3 3 30 'Where Juliet lives. And every cat and dog . . .'
Romeo considers himself brought lower than the animals because he cannot be near Juliet.

254/268	Creatures
260/263	Romeo

---

262   3 3 45 'Hadst thou no poison mixed, . . .'
This comment of Romeo's is echoed in several other places in the play. The
Apothecary's comments mark the end of the echo – but where did it begin?
(Hint: consider the Friar's first appearance.)

209/275   Plants

263   3 3 48 'O Friar, the damnèd use that word in hell.'
Romeo is still unable to control his passions. This is what dooms him, and it
is something which applies to many of the other characters who are dead by
the end of the play: Tybalt, Mercutio, Paris, Juliet. Try to work out what
'flaws' they had in their characters.

257/265   Passion
261/264   Romeo

264   3 3 65 'Thou canst not speak of that thou dost not feel.'
Romeo shares Juliet's frustration, in his case it is with the Friar, in her case it
it is with the Nurse. The young cannot seem to make the old understand
their impatience or sympathize with their passion. This is ironic when we
see how many of the adults in the play are ruled by their passions. What
motivates the Friar and the Nurse, if not passion?

221/293   Age
263/266   Romeo

265   3 3 71 'Taking the measure of an unmade grave.'
Compare this comment of Romeo's with a recent one of Juliet's. The last
scene, between Juliet and the Nurse, is closely paralleled by this scene
between Romeo and the Friar. We know in what ways Romeo and Juliet are
different, and what they have in common – but is this pattern matched by
the same symmetry between the characters of the Nurse and the Friar? What
have the Friar and the Nurse in common? (Hint: investigate the ways in
which they relate to the imagery and the themes which are important in the
play.)

263/268   Passion

266   3 3 106 'In what vile part of this anatomy . . .'
Romeo uses the same metaphor which Juliet did when she referred to 'the
mansion of love'. There are several places in the play where the lovers echo
each other's words. This technique more closely identifies them with each
other.

255/269   Aspects
          of style
264/276   Romeo
250/283   The body

267   3 3 109 'Art thou a man?'
What does this long, calm speech do for the pace of the play and why is its
appearance at this particular point in the action dramatically important? This
speech and the Friar's next one are important to the plot and they
summarize the basic themes of the play. Decide how far you think that the
Friar's scheme failed because of its basic weakness and how far because of
bad luck. Check how many of the play's themes and images, like fate, death,
love, disorder, animals, the body and fire are brought together here.

259/313   The Friar

268   3 3 111 'The unreasonable fury of a beast.'
This comment of the Friar's arises out of the Elizabethan view that animals
were frequently driven by passion, but never by reason. Animals did not
possess reason to the Elizabethan way of thinking. Which character in the
play is a personification of this idea? To a certain extent the next few lines in
the play suggest that this kind of passion is the main theme of the
play – rather than something else, like love.

261/275   Creatures
265/272   Passion

269   3 3 132 'Like powder in a skilless soldier's flask . . .'
The imagery of explosions returns here in the Friar's long speech. How prophetic does this comment of his turn out to be? Notice how often characters say things which have a prophetic ring to them. Why do you think Shakespeare included such things in his plays? Think about their effect on the way the play's characters seem to see and understand what is going on. Think also about their effect upon the audience, who frequently know more about what is actually going on than the characters in the play do.

266/271	Aspects of style	
247/277	Darkness and light	

270   3 3 159 'O Lord, I could have stayed here all the night . . .'
The Nurse's admiration for the Friar's fine words defuses the tenseness of the atmosphere for a moment. It also gives us an insight into the character of the Nurse; has she understood the Friar's advice in the same way that Romeo and Juliet have?

215/299	The Nurse

271   3 3 165 'How well my comfort is revived by this!'
Romeo is finally won over by the Friar, but as he leaves for his banishment we see, with the next scene, how Shakespeare at once accelerates the action in the play again but from another direction.

269/274	Aspects of style
248/273	Time

272   3 4 4 'And so did I. Well, we were born to die.'
Capulet appears to take Tybalt's death surprisingly calmly, and in the speech of Lady Capulet which follows it, it would seem that she too has overcome the violence of her first reaction. Has Tybalt's death brought them back to reality?

131/273	Lord Capulet
268/285	Passion

273   3 4 12 'Sir Paris, I will make a desperate tender . . .'
We can see that there has been a sudden change in Capulet's attitude to the proposed marriage. It could be that he is thinking that Paris is losing interest. This time it is Capulet's haste that brings the tragedy nearer, not the haste of Romeo or Juliet. Shakespeare emphasizes the sudden change in his mind. Compare Capulet's attitude now with his attitude when Paris first approached him seeking Juliet's hand in marriage.

272/291	Lord Capulet
271/276	Time

274   3 5 1 'Wilt thou be gone?'
The two lovers join in an aubade, which is a song greeting the dawn, usually sung by lovers in an opera after their wedding night. In French 'aube' means dawn. In Elizabethan poetry it was normal for such a song to be one of mourning, because the lovers now had to part.

271/278	Aspects of style

275   3 5 2 'It was the nightingale, . . .'
Juliet and Romeo now fear the coming daylight, represented here by the lark. The night is their friend, but it is the night of the nightingale not the raven which is their friend. One bird epitomizes the feelings of the love sonnet – the other the present. Likewise it is the pomegranate tree, not Romeo's sad sycamore of the first scene of the play, which is associated with their love now.

268/280	Creatures
262/315	Plants

276   3 5 6 'It was the lark . . .'
Haste has up to now been associated with Romeo's impetuous nature. From now on he is at peace and we will see a new maturity in him. Notice that

266/279	Romeo
273/290	Time

	Characters and ideas previous/next comment	

though the light of day is 'jocund' (merry, or pleasant), it is now associated with Romeo's death. The imagery of light is used to emphasize the contrast between night and day in the play. Night and day are used as symbols: for what?

---

277   3 5 13 'It is some meteor . . .'
Juliet tries to persuade Romeo that the light of the sun can still be their friend. Remember that so far in the play sunlight has been associated with hot passion; for example, remember Romeo's infatuation with Rosaline. Juliet wishes that the light were that of the night-time. The reference to meteors is appropriate because they were thought in Elizabethan times to be phenomena caused by gases escaping from the earth, which then ignited in the sky because of the heat of the sun.

269/281   Darkness and light

---

278   3 5 20 ''Tis but the pale reflex of Cynthia's brow.'
In mythology Cynthia, or Diana as she was also known, was the chaste and vindictive goddess of the moon and of the hunt.

274/282   Aspects of style

---

279   3 5 24 'Come, death, and welcome!'
Ironically, Romeo says he is prepared to die for love. It is ironic because fate has already acted to undermine their temporary happiness.

260/284   Fate
276/283   Romeo

---

280   3 5 29 'Some say the lark makes sweet division.'
Since the song of the lark represents the coming of day, and their separation, Juliet would prefer the song of the toad. Compare her use of animal imagery here with that we find in her 'fiery footed steeds' speech – notice how the same kind of imagery is used to create two quite different atmospheres.

275/311   Creatures
258/284   Juliet

---

281   3 5 36 'More light and light . . .'
See how many different themes of the play are involved in the symbolism of darkness and light. It is the use of the complicated imagery to do with light and dark which turns the peaceful atmosphere of this present scene to an atmosphere of anticipation, ready for the action to come.

277/364   Darkness and light

---

282   3 5 54 'O God, I have an ill-divining soul!'
This is reminiscent of the vision of 'untimely death' which Romeo had just before he met Juliet, but it is now Romeo who comforts Juliet. How have recent events affected Romeo's character? Has he changed at all? Both Romeo and Juliet are given visions of the future as the tragedy moves towards it climax. It is interesting to notice how the imagery of seeing and sight is used here in connection with the idea of 'seeing the future'. In the early part of the play seeing was connected with ideas about falling in love 'on sight'.

278/308   Aspects of style
258/286   Death and sickness

---

283   3 5 59 'Dry sorrow drinks our blood.'
The drinking image has now become a destructive one as the body itself is being consumed. This strengthens the growing power of the vision of death coming to 'consume' Juliet, both literally and sexually. The Elizabethans thought that sorrow was an emotion which literally consumed the blood, making people pale.

279/285   Romeo
266/314   The body

284 3 5 60 'O Fortune, Fortune!'
Fate was notoriously fickle, and these few lines of Juliet's would strike the audience as ironic.

279/288	Fate
280/287	Juliet

285 3 5 60 'O Fortune, Fortune!'
Romeo's leaving of Verona seems to mark an increasingly hostile mood in the play. Tybalt, Mercutio and Benvolio are all gone and Juliet seems to become very isolated. The Nurse appears to be much less supportive and Juliet's parents become aggressive and threatening.

272/297	Passion
283/342	Romeo

286 3 5 69 'Evermore weeping for your cousin's death?'
Lady Capulet's apparent callousness will tend to put the audience even more on the side of the lovers.

282/289	Death and sickness
238/293	Lady Capulet

287 3 5 81 'Villain and he be many miles asunder. –'
Up to now much of the irony has been dramatic irony, where the audience knows more than the characters. Here, in Juliet's speeches the double meanings are put into 'asides' and are intentional; the audience is meant to be in on Juliet's secret, but Lady Capulet is not. Notice how changed Juliet is from the girl we first met.

284/289	Juliet

288 3 5 93 'Indeed I never shall be satisfied . . .'
This comment of Juliet's is powerfully ironic–because we know how the story ends, and she does not.

284/294	Fate

289 3 5 96 'Madam, if you could find out but a man . . .'
Note how calm and mature Juliet seems when facing her mother. Although her talk of poison is a cover for her true feelings, it repeats an idea we have heard several times before. This speech of Juliet's raises again the difficult idea which occurs at several points in the play, that death can somehow be the supreme expression of love.

286/301	Death and sickness
287/290	Juliet

290 3 5 117 'Well, well, thou hast a careful father, . . .'
Compare this Juliet with the child of the first Act ('it is an honour that I dream not of'). Notice that it is the older characters who are now infected with haste.

289/292	Juliet
276/307	Time

291 3 5 126 'When the sun sets the earth doth drizzle dew, . . .'
This sustained metaphor of the sun, earth and sea seems a little out of place at this time. Capulet does not seem to feel much about Tybalt's death. Is this callousness on his part, or is he still too shocked to react?

273/295	Lord Capulet
254/292	The elements

292 3 5 131 'Thou conterfeitest a bark, . . .'
Capulet's words are ironic for it is he who, 20 lines further on, will unleash the storm. Again the sea imagery is used to emphasize the fickle nature of fate.

290/298	Juliet
291/335	The elements

*Characters and ideas
previous/next comment*

293   3 5 140 'I would the fool were married to her grave!'
The older characters are generally seen as cold, devious and hating. Is Lady
Capulet a parallel to Tybalt? Is cruelty the driving force of her character? The
extreme callousness of her remark will put the audience on the side of youth
against age.

264/295	Age
286/297	Lady Capulet

294   3 5 140 'I would the fool were married to her grave!'
The Elizabethans saw the curses of parents and of those who were dying as
being particularly ominous. This remark of Lady Capulet does of course
come tragically true.

288/319	Fate

295   3 5 149 'How, how, how, how, . . .'
Juliet has made a commendable effort not to offend her parents too much.
Capulet's contemptuous dismissal of her new independence of ideas seems
to show that she was only the 'hopeful lady of my earth' whilst she remained
a little girl, a dependant. Now that she is no longer a possession but is more
of a person in her own right, she represents a threat to his authority, a threat
which it seems he is not prepared to ignore.

293/300	Age
291/298	Lord Capulet

296   3 5 156 'Out, you green-sickness carrion!'
Notice Capulet's use of 'green'. This word is rare in *Romeo and Juliet*.
Compare this example with the way Romeo used the word when he first met
Juliet in her garden. At the start of the second scene in Act 2, Romeo
compares Juliet to sunlight. He says that the moon is envious because Juliet,
the moon's 'maid', 'is more fair than she'. Juliet is depicted as the moon's
'maid' because Romeo is comparing her to the mythical goddess Diana.
Romeo calls the moon 'sick and green' and Capulet calls Juliet 'green-
sickness carrion'.

229/304	Sight

297   3 5 157 'Fie, fie! What, are you mad?'
Lady Capulet now sees the feud for what it is; senseless passion which turns
to destroy those who cannot free themselves of it.

293/331	Lady Capulet
285/302	Passion

298   3 5 163 'Speak not, reply not, . . .'
Who else has been 'deaf to pleading' in this way? What parallel is being
subtly drawn between the two situations? (Hint: look at the Prince's
speeches.) Consider Romeo's banishment and the part in it which is played
by Prince Escalus. The authority of the head of State and the head of the
family were both seen as fundamental to social order in Elizabethan times.
Why then does Escalus's decision seem wise and Capulet's cruel? Bear in
mind that the Elizabethans would probably have seen Capulet's attitude as
highly reasonable.

292/301	Juliet
295/299	Lord Capulet

299   3 5 169 'You are to blame, my lord, . . .'
The Nurse is a trusted member of the Capulet household, but her attempt to
defend Juliet is answered with abuse by Capulet whose anger is directed
more at Juliet than at her. Parental authority in Elizabethan England tended
not to be open to negotiation!

298/300	Lord Capulet
270/303	The Nurse

300   3 5 190 'Look to't, think on't. I do not use to jest.'
Her parents cannot understand why Juliet does not think of love in terms of

295/385	Age

	Characters and ideas previous/next comment

a rich husband, and in their anger they threaten her with disinheritance. Have they forgotten about how it feels to be young and in love? Was Lady Capulet's marriage arranged for her? Does she love her husband, or does she see her marriage to him only in terms of wealth and 'a good match'?

299/307   Lord Capulet

301   3 5 203 'Talk not to me, . . .'
In her touching appeal, Juliet is horribly prophetic. Lady Capulet's reply is shocking, but from what you know of her character, do you think she really means it? Perhaps more importantly, why does Lady Capulet not take Juliet's terrible threat seriously?

289/312   Death and sickness
298/302   Juliet

302   3 5 206 'My husband is on earth, . . .'
The connection between the lovers and heaven is maintained. This prepares the way for their 'sacrifice' as 'saints'. Romeo has already spoken of Juliet (in the garden scene) in these religious terms.

301/305   Juliet
297/303   Passion

303   3 5 218 'I think it best you married with the County.'
The Nurse's advice may be misplaced but it is well-intentioned; she seems genuinely to think it is all for the best. (Do you believe that she is sincere?) Notice how Paris gets compared to an eagle, a bird of prey. The Nurse almost always agrees with whatever is the current opinion. Although the Nurse is probably only trying to please, her comments here serve to put even greater emphasis on Juliet's powerful love for Romeo.

302/306   Passion
299/305   The Nurse

304   3 5 221 'Hath not so green, so quick, . . .'
In view of the way this imagery has recently been used, how telling is this particular use of the word 'green' by the Nurse?

296/380   Sight

305   3 5 231 'Well, thou hast comforted me marvellous much.'
Unknown to her, this scene marks the Nurse's final conversation with Juliet. The Nurse does not seem to recognize how much Juliet has changed. Did Mercutio make a similar mistake in judging Romeo's character?

302/306   Juliet
303/321   The Nurse

306   3 5 231 'Well, thou hast comforted me marvellous much.'
From now on Juliet is very much her own woman. Her cool sarcasm about the Nurse shows an independence of mind beyond her years. Juliet has been deserted by everyone – she is becoming aware that fate has left her only one course of action.

305/309   Juliet
303/310   Passion

Act 4

307   4 1 2 'My father Capulet will have it so, . . .'
There seems to be no real reason for the haste of the proposed marriage, except Capulet's whim, and, therefore, it is bad luck. If it is true that he wants her to stop mourning Tybalt, as he believes she is doing, it is still an unlucky train of events which has caused the crisis.

300/318   Lord Capulet
290/316   Time

308   4 1 8 'For Venus smiles not in a house of tears.'
Paris's reference to Venus is more appropriate than he perhaps knows. Venus was the Roman goddess of love and she, says Paris, cannot be found in 'a house of tears'. This is word-play on 'house', because as well as meaning a dwelling-place it meant one of the twelve divisions of the Zodiac. Paris's comment therefore points up the influence of the stars again.

282/317	Aspects of style
100/309	Paris

309   4 1 18 'Happily met, my lady and my wife!'
This occasion is the only living meeting of Paris and Juliet. Compare it with the meetings of Romeo and Juliet, and notice that whilst Paris's conversations are formal and 'proper', Romeo's are passionate, almost reckless. Juliet is very self-possessed. Compare this with her first conversation with Romeo, when her verbal fencing quickly collapsed.

306/311	Juliet
308/310	Paris

310   4 1 35 'Thy face is mine, . . .'
Paris's idea of love is possessive, like Capulet's.

309/337	Paris
306/316	Passion

311   4 1 80 'Where serpents are.'
Juliet's bravery is instanced in her acceptance of serpents and bears. The idea of hiding with a dead man in his tomb is a frightening prophecy.

280/327	Creatures
309/312	Juliet

312   4 1 85 'And hide me with a dead man in his tomb−. . .'
In some editions of the play, 'shroud' is used here instead of 'tomb'. The choice often depends on whether the editor sees death as personalized in the play.

301/322	Death and sickness
311/313	Juliet

313   4 1 93 'Take thou this vial, . . .'
The Friar's plan, which he explains here, requires great courage of Juliet, and this increases our sympathy for her. Since the Friar's introduction into the play, we have been prepared for this moment. How much blame could we apportion to the Friar for the final tragedy?

312/315	Juliet
267/320	The Friar

314   4 1 94 'And this distilling liquor drink thou off; . . .'
The Friar's reference to drinking and drinks is another example of the mouth-drinking imagery. Notice where this imagery has arrived at: poison and death.

283/318	The body

315   4 1 99 'The roses in thy lips and cheeks shall fade . . .'
This is not the first time that roses have been connected with Juliet, but now they are fading.

313/316	Juliet
275/321	Plants

316   4 1 121 'Give me, give me! . . .'
The pace speeds up again because of the actions of the lovers. All the older people have now rejected Juliet, except the Friar, and he too will let her down by failing to get the letter through to Romeo and by being late to the tomb. He of all people knew when she would awaken. When the watch comes towards the tomb (and presumably his part in events would become known) the Friar runs away, deserting Juliet at the time of her greatest need.

315/321	Juliet
310/330	Passion
307/319	Time

Characters and ideas previous/next comment

317 4 2 1 'So many guests invite as here are writ . . .'
Again we see the bustle of family life used as a contrast with what has gone before and what is to come. Notice how effectively Shakespeare used this simple device in the play.

308/322	Aspects of style

318 4 2 2 'Sirrah, go hire me twenty cunning cooks.'
Capulet needs twenty cooks. He has forgotten that because of Tybalt's death they must not 'revel much'. His love of high living seems stronger than his other feelings. After the atmosphere of haste and fear in the last scene, this homely exchange forms an effective contrast.

307/328	Lord Capulet
314/324	The body

319 4 2 24 'I'll have this knot knit up tomorrow morning.'
The moving of the marriage date is important. It ruins the Friar's plan. There is no real reason to bring the marriage forward yet another day. Fate seems to be leaving nothing to chance.

294/323	Fate
316/327	Time

320 4 2 31 'Now, afore God, . . .'
Capulet's praise of the Friar is ironic in view of his hand in the coming tragedy.

313/333	The Friar

321 4 3 1 'Ay, those attires are best.'
Juliet continues to show amazing self-control. She is now completely isolated from all support. Although present, the Nurse says nothing. This is very unusual: the Nurse's normal behaviour is to be constantly chattering. Why does she stay silent here? The next time she speaks it will be over Juliet's body. Juliet's comment at line seven is very ironic, and her calmness and determination are both impressive and sad in one so young.

316/322	Juliet
315/339	Plants
305/328	The Nurse

322 4 3 14 'Farewell! God knows when we shall meet again.'
The courage and isolation of Juliet is emphasized in this speech. Compare her doubts about the Friar's potion with Romeo's doubt about the one he buys from the Apothecary. Such parallels in the play are very common, especially towards the end.

317/325	Aspects of style
312/331	Death and sickness
321/323	Juliet

323 4 3 20 'Come, vial.'
Does it matter that, later on, no one seems to notice the phial or the dagger and suspect the truth? Is it not a little too contrived that all the other characters jump so quickly to the wrong conclusion? The answer is that in an actual performance, no one in the audience ever seems to notice. This is because the play was written by a person who envisaged how it would work when it was performed on a stage. Why should Juliet be more worried at this point in the play about waking up before Romeo gets to the tomb?

319/343	Fate
322/324	Juliet

324 4 3 34 'To whose foul mouth no healthsome air breathes in, . . .'
In Juliet's fevered imagination her previous use of images is distorted to produce a change in the way she uses them. The body will die, the mouth of the vault will be 'foul', and no pleasant flowers will come to mind, but only the fearful mandrake plant. Juliet's speech prepares us for the terror of the Capulet tomb. Notice how accurately she foresees the future. When has she done this before?

166/342	Dreams
323/332	Juliet
318/326	The body

	Characters and ideas	
	previous/next comment	

325   4 3 47 'And shrieks like mandrakes torn out of the earth, . . .'
The shape of the root of the mandrake plant often appears to resemble a man's legs. The Elizabethans thought that the roots of this plant drove men mad with their screams as they were torn up from the ground.

322/327	Aspects of style

326   4 3 59 'Here's drink. I drink to thee.'
The image of Juliet drinking the poison as a toast to Romeo is full of irony. Her action echoes all the occasions in the play when drink and drinking have been mentioned, but gives new meaning to them by changing the focus of the imagery. This constant 'reworking' of the imagery into more subtle forms is one example of Shakespeare's great skill with language.

324/327	The body

327   4 4 1 'Hold, take these keys . . .'
The trifling domestic problems of the Capulets provide a contrast to the dramatic scene to follow. Shakespeare contrasts the busy, bustling world of the Capulets preparing a wedding feast with the stillness and silence of Juliet. Notice how cleverly food and eating connect the two scenes in a rather bizarre but effective way. Notice also how the animal imagery is used. How different to the first dawn is this second 'dawn' in the play?

325/328	Aspects of style
311/348	Creatures
326/353	The body
319/329	Time

328   4 4 5 'Look to the baked meats, good Angelica.'
Angelica is Shakespeare's brilliantly ironic name for the Nurse. Notice how Capulet is friendly to the Nurse again now that he thinks he is getting his own way.

327/332	Aspects of style
318/334	Lord Capulet
321/330	The Nurse

329   4 5 1 'Mistress! What, mistress! . . .'
From now onwards there will be many changes of atmosphere, pace and scene in rapid succession until the Friar stands in the tomb at the end of the play. What dramatic effect does this constant, blinding acceleration of the action produce? Think about the role of fate in the play and about what has been said about the relentlessness of the succession of events.

327/345	Time

330   4 5 5 'Sleep for a week. For . . .'
Whatever fears the Nurse may have had, she is now her old cheerful self again and once more talking about sex. Notice how cleverly this apparent relaxation of the tension actually serves to heighten it for us.

316/346	Passion
328/0	The Nurse

331   4 5 20 'Revive, look up, or I will die with thee!'
In spite of what she says, it takes more than this to kill Lady Capulet. But compare this with Lady Montague's reaction to Romeo's exile.

322/332	Death and sickness
297/397	Lady Capulet

332   4 5 28 'Death lies on her like an untimely frost . . .'
In Capulet's speech, how appropriate are the images of plants and stillness, bearing in mind the person who gave Juliet the potion? In what ways could we agree with Capulet that 'life' has been separated from Juliet? Are they the same ways which he has in mind, do you think? What effective dramatic technique is Shakespeare using here that he has used again and again throughout the rest of the play?

328/336	Aspects of style
331/333	Death and sickness
324/391	Juliet

Notice how Shakespeare stops this scene being as tragic as the tomb scene later on. This is important, because the play's ending would not be so effective if Shakespeare tried to lift this climax too high or hold it for long, or if he had two equally powerful climaxes in the action. In this play the greatest tragedy and climax must come at the very end of the action, if it is to produce its most powerful impact.

---

333   4 5 33 'Come, is the bride ready to go to church?'
This comment from the Friar is important. It emphasizes the tragedy that Juliet has died on what they thought would be the happiest day of her life. In addition, the comment echoes a powerful and chilling theme in the imagery of the play. Can you identify it?

332/334	Death and sickness
320/338	The Friar

---

334   4 5 35 'O son, the night before thy wedding day . . .'
Capulet uses the image of Death as Juliet's lover. This is a powerful medieval image which is used frequently throughout the play. His next comment is ironically true; his son-in-law will soon be dead.

333/337	Death and sickness
328/340	Lord Capulet

---

335   4 5 41 'Have I thought long to see this morning's face, . . .'
Many of the themes and images are combined in confusion, as with Juliet when we heard her last; daytime is hated and sight is abhorrent to them because all it shows them is death.

292/382	The elements

---

336   4 5 49 'O woe! O woeful, woeful, woeful day!'
Look carefully at the next three speeches. How does Shakespeare avoid a genuinely tragic atmosphere?

332/340	Aspects of style

---

337   4 5 56 'Most detestable Death, . . .'
Paris takes up the image of Death as Juliet's lover. How will it soon apply to him?

334/338	Death and sickness
310/360	Paris

---

338   4 5 65 'Peace, ho, for shame!'
The Friar's speech at this point emphasizes to us the unreality of Juliet's death. Interestingly, much of what he says would have been just as appropriate if she were really dead. This is cleverly constructed by Shakespeare. Look at the use of language by the Friar, and think about what implications we can draw, depending upon whether characters use prose or poetry in their speeches.

337/346	Death and sickness
333/343	The Friar

---

339   4 5 79 'Dry up your tears and stick . . .'
This is a beautifully subtle reminder to the audience. Who else has been linked with rosemary, and when?

321/349	Plants

---

340   4 5 84 'All things that we ordainèd festival . . .'
Again, contrasting or contradictory images are used to highlight the confusion in a character's mind, as was the case with Romeo in the first scene of the play and again, with Juliet, after she had heard of Tybalt's death.

336/341	Aspects of style
334/403	Lord Capulet

---

341   4 5 96 'Faith, we may put up our pipes and be gone.'
This comic interlude would seem to come at a rather inappropriate time in
the action of the play. But remember the audience knows that Juliet is not
really dead. What then is the dramatic purpose of this scene?

340/347	Aspects of style

Act 5

342   5 1 1 'If I may trust the flattering truth . . .'
This dream of Romeo's is indeed a prophecy. What he says is heavy with
dramatic irony; the audience knows the true situation but Romeo does not.

324/371	Dreams
285/344	Romeo

343   5 1 18 'Her body sleeps in Capel's monument, . . .'
The Friar was supposed to have given the news to Romeo's servant,
Balthasar. What two things have gone wrong with the Friar's plan so far?
Could either have been avoided?

323/344	Fate
338/358	The Friar

344   5 1 24 'Is it e'en so? Then I defy you, stars!'
Romeo defies fate to do any worse to him; he will now fight against being
'fortune's fool'. Romeo is even more impetuous now that he thinks Juliet is
dead. It is this haste which, at this point in the plot, makes the tragedy
certain. However, love has matured Romeo, as it has Juliet, and he is
planning calmly and clearly.

343/355	Fate
342/345	Romeo

345   5 1 30 'Leave me and do the thing I bid thee do.'
Romeo seems to have matured quickly – he seems calm and sure of purpose.
He no longer seeks out the advice of others, and seems to have none of the
doubts he was plagued with at the start of the play.

344/351	Romeo
329/352	Time

346   5 1 34 'Well, Juliet, I will lie with thee tonight.'
The themes of love and death meet here. Consider the number of possible
different meanings of 'lie with'.

338/348	Death and sickness
330/351	Passion

347   5 1 37 'I do remember an apothecary, . . .'
It is important that an explanation is offered for the ease with which Romeo
is able to obtain poison. The pitifully poor Apothecary is a clever solution.
Notice how Shakespeare makes full use of the actual scene later on, to reflect
upon what really is poisonous in the lives of people.

341/357	Aspects of style

348   5 1 40 'Culling of simples. Meagre were his looks.'
The human body has been associated with many things in the play; here it is
associated with death, as are the ugly reptiles and fishes.

327/350	Creatures
346/353	Death and sickness

349   5 1 40 'Culling of simples. Meagre were his looks.'
Notice how closely the old Apothecary, described here by Romeo, parallels
the Friar as a character in the play. A modern director might almost be
tempted to cast them as the same actor to emphasize this. How closely does

339/362	Plants

the imagery associated with the Friar (plants, herbs and the laws of Nature) relate to that associated with the Apothecary? Notice how this imagery of Nature's laws, of new growth, buds, (de)flowering and decay is very closely related to the imagery of death in the play.

---

350   5 1 42 'And in his needy shop a tortoise hung, . . .'
In this speech of Romeo's, what do the animals he mentions tell us about the atmosphere of the Apothecary's shop? What do they suggest about the Apothecary and his trade?

348/377   Creatures

---

351   5 1 52 'Here lives a caitiff wretch . . .'
Has Romeo's new maturity made him more sensitive towards other people? His obvious sympathy with this poor wretch and his pathetic stock, reveals a side to his character which we have not seen before. Notice that Romeo had already thought of buying poison.

345/355   Romeo
346/352   Passion

---

352   5 1 58 'Come hither, man. I see that thou art poor.'
Here in the shop of the Apothecary we see that the imagery of explosions, haste and death meet in this speech of Romeo's. Where else in the play can this kind of mixture be found?

351/360   Passion
345/381   Time

Look at the imagery that is used by the Friar when Romeo and Juliet meet to be married by him in the sixth scene of Act 2. Notice the similarities of tone and imagery between that scene and this one. Both scenes are turning points in the action of the play.

---

353   5 1 63 'And that the trunk may be discharged of breath . . .'
Notice how the references to the human body are used in the imagery. Romeo's body is reduced to a trunk, and the womb is now associated with death, not life.

327/356   The body
348/354   Death and
sickness

---

354   5 1 68 'Art thou so bare and full of wretchedness . . .'
Look carefully at this description of the Apothecary by Romeo. The language is full of subtle echoes of many of the themes in the play: food, drink, the colour of the face, the light (or lack of it) in someone's eyes, the support of friends, the laws of the world, the laws of nature, the essence of real wealth, or riches and happiness. These ideas and themes are explored through the imagery and other characters in the play. Exactly who *is* the Apothecary? Does he remind you of any other 'character' in the play? (No, not the Friar, if you were thinking of him, although that is a good parallel.)

353/356   Death and
sickness

The Apothecary and the Friar are related through their connection with the world of plants. The Friar sees 'good and evil' both in plants and in men. The Apothecary is even-handed in the way he dispenses cures and poisons made from nature. Both characters, in their own ways, are agents of death for Romeo and Juliet, although in some ways they can both claim to be innocent of causing the tragedy; they were only trying to help. The Apothecary is an agent of, or a personification of, the 'character' of Death in the play. Look at some of the words Romeo uses to describe him and his shop: meagre, famine, starvation, contempt, beggary, full of wretchedness. He is surrounded by an alligator, skins of ill-shaped fishes, bladders, musty seeds and remnants. Romeo cannot understand why someone who is so pitiful, whom 'misery had worn . . . to the bones', does not prefer death as being better than life.

The Friar is a much more subtle agent, or personification, of Death; not because of his appearance but, like the Apothecary in his shop, because of the things which surround him, the powers he has and the chaos which he (perhaps unwittingly) unleashes on the world of Mantua.

---

355   5 1 72 'The world is not thy friend, . . .'

Romeo's own misfortune has made him aware of the suffering of others. He sees that for the Apothecary 'the world is not thy friend, nor the world's law'. Ironically, this is also very true of Romeo and Juliet. How much of the eventual tragedy is due to their 'star-crossed' fate, and how much to the unfriendliness of 'the world's law'?

| 351/365 | Romeo |
| 344/358 | Fate |

---

356   5 1 77 'Put this in any liquid thing you will . . .'

The food imagery has changed. It is now death, not wine, that will be drunk; no longer will there be a toast at the wedding feast.

| 354/366 | Death and sickness |
| 353/367 | The body |

---

357   5 1 80 'There is thy gold – worse poison to men's souls, . . .'

Does this speech show a maturer, more wistful side of Romeo? Is there a clue here to the reason for the feud between the Montagues and the Capulets?

| 347/359 | Aspects of style |

Look at the end of this Act, where Montague and Capulet make promises about what they will do to make amends. How ironic is the comment Romeo makes in his speech here about gold? Consider whether it is a fair criticism of the values of Montague and Capulet.

---

358   5 2 1 'Holy Franciscan Friar, brother, ho!'

Friar John's delay would seem reasonable to Shakespeare's audience. There had been a recent outbreak of plague in London. Was this delay just another example of 'unhappy fortune' or had the Friar made a mistake?

| 343/389 | The Friar |
| 355/359 | Fate |

---

359   5 2 14 'I could not send it – . . .'

This confession by Friar John is sometimes pointed to as another one of the play's very 'convenient' coincidences. Some critics feel that Shakespeare relied too heavily on coincidence, especially in *Romeo and Juliet*. Interestingly, these supposed flaws in the play's structure are rarely perceived by audiences watching performances, in which case it is debateable whether or not they are flaws.

| 358/363 | Fate |
| 357/360 | Aspects of style |

---

360   5 3 8 'As signal that thou hearest something approach.'

Paris begins to speak of his sadness at Juliet's death. Ironically, what he says in the next few lines, and his use of plant imagery, is a parallel of what we heard from Romeo when we first met him in Act 1. Both characters speak in a rather formal, affected way in rhyming couplets, which lack the sincerity and dignity of, for example, Juliet's poetry. Paris conforms to the conventional stereotype of an Elizabethan suitor, although this does not mean that he is necessarily insincere. Paris in Act 5 is rather like the early Romeo, but Romeo is by now much changed. Paris, the rival lover, brings flowers to the tomb of Juliet; there to meet with Death, the other rival lover.

337/362	Paris
359/361	Aspects of style
352/366	Passion

---

361   5 3 12 'Sweet flower, with flowers thy bridal bed I strew – . . .'

Paris comes to speak a short elegy over Juliet; a poem lamenting the dead. It is a simple rhymed pattern of blank verse and is another example of the way

| 360/364 | Aspects of style |

Shakespeare adjusted the pattern and style of the language to suit the situation.

---

362   5 3 12 'Sweet flower, with flowers thy bridal bed I strew—...'
We see something of Paris's character here; he seems gentle, compassionate and genuinely upset about Juliet's death.

360/363   Paris
349/0   Plants

---

363   5 3 19 'What cursèd foot wanders this way tonight . . .'
Notice the double irony in what Paris says here. Whose is the 'cursed foot' which has wandered into the graveyard, his or Romeo's? How true is it that Romeo was 'cursed' from the start, and that he was doomed by fate all along?

362/364   Paris
359/365   Fate

---

364   5 3 21 'What, with a torch? Muffle me, night, awhile.'
This incident is an ironic parallel to that other night-time meeting between Romeo and Juliet in her garden.

363/369   Paris
281/373   Darkness
　　　　　and light
361/369   Aspects
　　　　　of style

---

365   5 3 23 'Hold, take this letter.'
If Romeo had not insisted on Balthasar's going away, the tragedy might still have been averted. How?

355/366   Romeo
363/372   Fate

---

366   5 3 28 'Why I descend into this bed of death . . .'
Romeo's words produce the image of Death as a lover, married to Juliet.

Remember what the Friar said to Romeo at his wedding, that 'violent delights have violent ends and in their triumph die', and that 'Too swift arrives as tardy as too slow'. Was the Friar right?

365/370   Romeo
360/368   Passion
356/367   Death and
　　　　　sickness

---

367   5 3 45 'Thou detestable maw, thou womb of death, . . .'
The body and food are once again associated with death.

366/368   Death and
　　　　　sickness
356/374   The body

---

368   5 3 55 'Can vengeance be pursued further than death?'
Paris speaks the play's final question. Do you think that the feud will be pursued after the lovers' deaths?

366/380   Passion
367/375   Death and
　　　　　sickness

---

369   5 3 70 'Wilt thou provoke me? Then have at thee, boy!'
Why is the death of Paris so necessary for the play to work properly? In Paris's death we see the triumph of the love of Romeo and Juliet; honest, passionate, innocent. They were not tainted with the worldly considerations which others attached to marriage, like money, position, status, respectability and 'the proper thing'. Paris's continued presence would have left a complication in the plot, a loose end, a blurring of the outcome of the play.

364/370   Paris
364/370   Aspects
　　　　　of style

---

370   5 3 74 'In faith, I will. Let me peruse this face.'
Ironically this is the first time that Paris and Romeo have actually met; and, as in the past, Romeo tries unsuccessfully to walk away from a fight. Throughout the play we can find many examples of 'opposite' characters meeting like this.

In some ways the play's action proceeds entirely by confrontation, not by the telling of a tale or by the rise to (or fall from) grace of a powerful central figure.

369/0	Paris
366/375	Romeo
369/372	Aspects of style

371   5 3 80 'Or am I mad, . . .
At this point Romeo cannot tell what is real from what is dream-like. This blurring of the boundaries of what is real begins Romeo's greatest, and final, speech in the play. We see a powerful fusing of the imagery at the tragedy's climax. This is brilliantly appropriate, because much of the action of the play takes place in the half-worlds between sleeping and waking; remember Mercutio's 'Queen Mab' speech, the meeting of Romeo and Juliet in the garden, the 'false death' of Juliet.

| 342/387 | Dreams |

372   5 3 82 'One writ with me in sour misfortunes's book.'
Romeo is calm enough to feel pity for Paris who, like him, has had his name written in the book of fate. Like Mercutio and Tybalt before him, he seems to be too single-minded, too 'star-crossed' to survive.

| 370/381 | Aspects of style |
| 365/379 | Fate |

373   5 3 90 'A lightning before death.'
Notice how the imagery of the play strikes through the action. Even though 'dead', Juliet is still the source of all light to Romeo. This imagery of 'lightning' was introduced earlier in the play by Juliet and this is an effective echo of it. Can you recall where she introduced it?

Look at the scene in the moonlight in her garden, in the second scene of Act 2. Her premonitions are well-echoed in this word-play of Romeo's. The imagery of light returns in its final form; a sudden violent discharge of passion in the midst of a storm. Like the love of Romeo and Juliet, it leaps between earth and heaven and, by its very existence, destroys itself and all that it touches.

| 364/376 | Darkness and light |

374   5 3 92 'Death, that hath sucked the honey of thy breath, . . .'
Again Death is portrayed as feeding on life. This is the third, and final, reference to sucking in the play. Why does this imagery appear at the climax of the tragedy?

| 367/378 | The body |

375   5 3 94 'Thou art not conquered.'
This is the supreme irony of the play. Romeo sees the colour starting to return to Juliet's lips and cheeks, but does not recognize it for what it is. At the very instant when life begins to return to Juliet, Romeo kills himself in desolation at losing her to Death. Within sixty lines she is asking for him by name.

| 368/377 | Death and sickness |
| 370/380 | Romeo |

376   5 3 95 'Is crimson in thy lips and in thy cheeks, . . .'
Fire and paleness, as in the play's imagery of the dawn, have at last met in this final irony; Juliet is Life in Death.

| 373/380 | Darkness and light |

| | | *Characters and ideas previous/next comment* |

377 5 3 102 'Why art thou yet so fair?'
The ancient and powerful image of Death the lover now joins Romeo in this final moment of passion.

| 375/379 | Death and sickness |
| 350/388 | Creatures |

378 5 3 110 'Will I set up my everlasting rest . . .'
Here in the play's final darkness we see a concentration on the imaginative, spiritual side of the body. The life/death-giving drive, which began the play with physical violence, has been transformed into an image of the body at its most mysterious when in death.

| 374/383 | The body |

379 5 3 111 'And shake the yoke of inauspicious stars . . .'
The only way that Romeo can now see to throw off his fate is to die, and be rid of it.

| 377/397 | Death and sickness |
| 372/384 | Fate |

380 5 3 111 'And shake the yoke of inauspicious stars . . .'
Romeo sees that his stars and fate have brought him to this point; the imagery of light has built towards this point with great consistency. Notice how it is sight, but not love, which is extinguished by death.

376/386	Darkness and light
375/382	Romeo
368/393	Passion
304/0	Sight

381 5 3 115 'A dateless bargain to engrossing death!'
Romeo and Juliet's love will now transcend time. It will become a 'dateless bargain' struck with death. Bearing in mind the way contrasting themes and images have been used so extensively in the play, it seems quite in keeping that the price of their immortality is death. This seemingly contradictory idea is actually very common in the literature of many cultures in the world. In the case of Romeo and Juliet, was this fate inevitable?

| 352/382 | Time |
| 372/384 | Aspects of style |

382 5 3 117 'Thou desperate pilot, . . .'
This is another reference to Romeo's 'pilot'. In *Romeo and Juliet* elements like the sea are used to symbolize fate. Compare this reference to the elements and the sea with Romeo's words immediately before the feast where he meets Juliet (end of scene four in Act 1). Who has been Romeo's 'pilot' through this tragedy?

There is plenty of evidence to make a good case that Romeo's 'pilot' was either Love, or Death (in the role of Fate). Romeo's speeches suggest that he recognizes both.

Romeo has been destroyed by Fate. The dramatic tension here is caused by the fact that we, the audience, know that Juliet could awaken at any second. Romeo's impetuous haste seems to be the final undoing of him, to our eyes anyway. Has this been the case all along?

380/394	Romeo
335/400	The elements
381/385	Time

383 5 3 119 'Here's to my love!' (*He drinks*)
Here, as Romeo drinks the Apothecary's potion, the drinking imagery has come full circle from life and joy at the feast, to this point of death and tragedy.

| 378/392 | The body |

	Characters and ideas *previous/next comment*

384   5 3 120 'Thy drugs are quick. Thus with a kiss I die.'
Romeo dies moments before Juliet awakens. Does it seem too coincidental that this should happen? Shakespeare's skill as a dramatist is confirmed by the fact that audiences do not see the event as just too pat to be acceptable, but rather they see it as a finely balanced moment of great tension.

379/389   Fate
381/387   Aspects
          of style

Romeo is a true, unthinking romantic at this point. He accepts the situation as would a child. He has little command over his emotions. This is symptomatic of his behaviour at other places in the play.

385   5 3 121 'Saint Francis be my speed!'
It often seems in the play that impetuous haste is the cause of all the tragedy. But if you look more closely, for example here at the entrance of the Friar, you will see that haste is only the way Fate turns its intentions into reality. The tragedy is not the fault of the Friar's arriving just after Romeo has taken poison; the lovers were 'star-crossed' from the first.

300/397   Age
 382/0   Time

386   5 3 125 'What torch is yond . . .'
This passing reference by the Friar to the torchlight which he can see in the Capulet's monument, is more important than it at first seems. The imagery of light and fire, so revealing in the play so far, and so closely connected with the lovers, is now connected only with the tomb, with death.

380/396   Darkness
          and light

387   5 3 137 'As I did sleep under this yew tree here . . .'
Balthasar only thought he was dreaming. Could this help us to understand the role of the other dreams mentioned in the play?

 371/0   Dreams
384/390   Aspects
          of style

388   5 2 151 'I hear some noise. Lady, come from that nest . . .'
Shakespeare's irony is often subtle. Notice the Friar's use of 'nest' in connection with Juliet . . . 'Lady, come from that nest of death, contagion, and unnatural sleep'. Now compare it with the Nurse's use of the word, also in connection with Juliet, at the end of the fifth scene in Act 2 . . . 'your love must climb a bird's nest soon when it is dark'. The Nurse's meaning is sexual; Romeo will climb the ladder to nest with Juliet. The Friar's usage relates instead, and for his part unconsciously, to the imagery of Death the sexual paramour.

 377/0   Creatures

389   5 3 153 'A greater power than we can contradict . . .'
How do these two lines sum up an important theme of the play? What is the 'greater power' that the Friar speaks of: fate, love or death?

358/391   The Friar
 384/0   Fate

390   5 3 155 'Thy husband in thy bosom there lies dead; . . .'
This sad moment forms another of the play's many brilliant symmetries. Fate forces Romeo to die with Paris, just as it forced Tybalt to die with Mercutio. What dramatic effect do these parallels have?

387/400   Aspects
          of style

391   5 3 160 'Go, get thee hence, for I will not away.'
Juliet's willpower has enabled her to defy her family. Her last expression of

389/401   The Friar

	Characters and ideas previous/next comment

character is her defiance of the Friar who, like everybody else, has also let her down.

332/393	Juliet

392   5 3 161 'What's here? A cup, . . .
This is the last reference to drinking in the play. Compare this mention of 'cup' by Juliet with the servant's talk of a 'cup of wine' in the second scene of Act 1. The semi-religious imagery of wine and drinking in the play rises again here, in another of the many ironies and parallels.

383/399	The body

393   5 3 169 'Yea, noise? Then I'll be brief. O happy dagger!'
Juliet has always been the more practical and courageous of the two lovers. Her suicide is only one of several examples of which you should be aware. A dagger is more savage than poison, and demands more courage in use; it implies greater commitment, the overcoming of a greater fear of death, and therefore its use evokes more pity. That is why Romeo takes poison and *then* Juliet stabs herself; hers is the traditional, noble and glorious death of the warrior who is vanquished, but who will not be enslaved.

391/394	Juliet
380/402	Passion

394   5 3 170 'This is thy sheath . . .'
Were Romeo and Juliet surrounded by well-meaning people all along? To us the only 'crime' of the lovers was to love each other. But to the Elizabethans a secret marriage without parental consent was an extremely serious act of social disobedience which violated important cultural norms.

382/406	Romeo
393/406	Juliet

395   5 3 170 'This is thy sheath . . .'
Then, as now, the Church saw suicide as a sin; the Friar has been skating on very thin ice in helping the lovers. However, the love of Romeo and Juliet is a kind of salvation for them – like true saints, their love has somehow overcome death. The climax of the play shows death itself as subject to the power of love.

393/402	Passion

396   5 3 171 'This is the place. There, where the torch doth burn.'
The Page's observation is important. Bearing in mind the role which the imagery of light has in the play, do you find it ironic that it should be here in the tomb that 'the torch' burns?

386/408	Darkness and light

397   5 3 206 'O me! This sight of death is as a bell . . .'
Lady Capulet has already said that she is comparatively young. Is this genuine emotion over Juliet's death on her part, or just more self-pity? Compare Lady Montague's reaction with that of Lady Capulet's when she heard about Tybalt's death: the difference explains a lot about their respective characters.

385/398	Age
379/398	Death and sickness
331/0	Lady Capulet
24/0	Lady Montague

398   5 3 210 'Alas, my liege, my wife is dead tonight!'
Of the six deaths in the play, all except that of Lady Montague are of young people. This is not accidental. Consider what the play is about.

397/0	Death and sickness
397/0	Age

399   5 3 216 'Seal up the mouth of outrage . . .'
The Prince uses the 'mouth' imagery of the tomb, but he seems also to be

392/0	The body

		Characters and ideas *previous/next comment*

talking about the way too many sacrifices have been made to death. Which 'outrage' do you think he has in mind?

---

400   5 3 217 'Till we can clear these ambiguities . . .'
The play and its imagery have been full of 'ambiguities' which the deaths of the lovers will clarify.

390/401	Aspects of style
382/0	The elements

---

401   5 3 223 'I am the greatest, able to do least, . . .'
Look carefully at what the Friar has to say for himself here. How ironic is what he says? The Friar's speech at the tomb is a kind of Chorus – an epilogue.

391/0	The Friar
400/402	Aspects of style

---

402   5 3 292 'See what a scourge is laid upon your hate, . . .'
Love has proved stronger than hatred, stronger even than death. But to what extent is the play almost as much about hatred as about love?

401/407	Aspects of style
395/404	Passion

---

403   5 3 294 'And I, for winking at your discords . . .'
How far are the Capulets more to blame for the tragedy than the Montagues? Which of the two families is the more punished?

0/405	Lord Montague
340/405	Lord Capulet

---

404   5 3 295 'And I, for winking at your discords . . .'
Love has acted to teach society a lesson. Love has shown itself to be stronger than even the power of fate. This moral is something which people should take to heart in their dealings with each other; it seems to be the message of the play.

402/0	Passion

---

405   5 3 296 'O brother Montague, give me thy hand.'
Capulet is generous to the last, and is the first to offer his hand. How consistent is his character as a kindly parent? Or is Capulet the guiltier of the two heads of houses in sowing the seeds of the tragedy? Notice that their gold is all the Capulets and Montagues have left now.

403/0	Lord Capulet
403/0	Lord Montague

---

406   5 3 296 'O brother Montague, give me thy hand.'
We knew from the start of the play that Romeo and Juliet would die, but their end holds hope for the future: their deaths, like that of saints, have saved the lives of others. This complex sanctifying, purifying imagery starts to grow when Romeo and Juliet first meet. The ultimate triumph of the love of Romeo and Juliet is that it was a love which did not listen to advice. And by not allowing their deaths to occur at the actual end of the play, Shakespeare turns this into an optimistic play; the lovers have not died in vain.

In these last few speeches of the play, we see that Romeo and Juliet are finally safe from the ravages of fate and accident. Now, when the lovers' view of the world is at its most separate from that of the rest of the characters, the power of love brings about a complete change in the world.

394/0	Romeo
394/0	Juliet

---

407   5 3 305 'A glooming peace this morning with it brings.'
The play makes, amongst other things, a political point; society depends upon order and authority. The Prince represents these abstractions.

402/0	Aspects of style

Characters and ideas previous/next comment

Compare his three appearances and you will see that the symmetries are striking. Romeo and Juliet is a play of contrasts, of checks and balances, of opposites. The Capulets reflect the Montagues; Juliet and Romeo are their only children; the Nurse and Mercutio their closest friends; Tybalt contrasts with Benvolio, and so on.

More than half of the play is set in rhyme and this gives the drama the quality of an extended dramatic poem.

---

408   5 3 306 'The sun for sorrow will not show his head.'
The feud ends in darkness; light belonged to the young lovers.

396/0   Darkness and light

Characters in the play

Benvolio

Benvolio's opening words, 'Part, fools', are typical of the man who sometimes seems to exist in the play as a living contrast to other characters. He is a peace-keeper as opposed to the aggressive Tybalt; his prosaic utterances contrast with Mercutio's brilliant word-play; his caution shows up Romeo's impetuosity; his word is trusted by both Montague and the Prince. And yet he tells Lady Montague he has a 'troubled mind' and a 'weary self'; is he perhaps an introvert awash in a sea of extroverts?

Lord Capulet

Capulet is a difficult character to assess, since his behaviour appears so contradictory. Perhaps it is his true character which we see in his autocratic treatment of Juliet when she opposes his will, and his loving words earlier are merely for appearance's sake. He has married a woman much younger than himself, and it is possible that he may see his wife and daughter as possessions, like the wealth to which he so often refers.

Lady Capulet

Lady Capulet has married a much older man (as she points out several times!), and seems to thinks of marriage as a career which must be carefully planned to be profitable. She seems to have no real relationship with her daughter, but relies on the Nurse whom, nevertheless, she finds irritating. After Juliet's appeal, 'cast me not away', falls on deaf ears, we feel no sympathy for Lady Capulet. Even at the end of the play it is her own 'sepulchre' she is thinking of.

The Friar

The Friar is an important person in the story because he is the ally of Romeo and Juliet, and it is his plot which miscarries and hastens the final tragedy. He is portrayed as a kindly, unworldly – perhaps too unworldly – man. He is too optimistic about his plan, and in hoping that the marriage will bring the families together, but his intentions are always good. He may even have been correct about the marriage settling the feud.

Gregory and Sampson

Gregory and Sampson only appear once in the play, as far as the stage-directions are concerned, but they are important in setting the scene for the feuding, and in underlining the atmosphere of violence in Verona. Like all good comedy duos each is a foil to the other. Sampson is the boastful one, and Gregory, who obviously feels that he is superior, gets his amusement from puncturing Sampson's self-esteem.

Juliet

At the beginning Juliet, who is not quite fourteen years old, is even more childishly obedient and inexperienced than we might expect from someone her age. However, after she has fallen in love, she shows herself to be practical, determined and independent. Her development is sudden but complete. She is utterly loyal to Romeo, and defies the whole world for him. We not only feel sympathy for Juliet, but respect as well.

Mercutio

Mercutio makes his appearance comparatively late in the play, after we have met most of the major characters. His lively, bawdy wit and brilliantly lyrical imagination burst onto the scene, to contrast with the melancholy Romeo and sensible Benvolio. He lives intensely, never stops talking and does not suffer fools gladly. He dies cursing both the Capulets and the Montagues; he cannot seem to take either life or death seriously.

Lord Montague

Montague shows much more concern for his son than Capulet does for his daughter. At the beginning Montague is worried about Romeo's behaviour, not for any selfish reason, but because he thinks Romeo may do himself some harm. It is perhaps not surprising, therefore, that Romeo's second thought, after questioning Balthasar about the safety of Juliet, was for his father.

Lady Montague

Lady Montague is much more concerned about her husband and son, than Lady Capulet is with her family. Lady Montague's first words are to restrain her husband from fighting, which she does calmly but firmly. Her next speech shows her care for Romeo; in the end she dies of grief because of Romeo's exile. She is an interesting contrast to Lady Capulet.

The Nurse

The Nurse is a close and trusted member of the Capulet household; her position is far superior to that of a normal servant and she knows it, as we can tell from her rather bossy attitude to Peter, the servant. Juliet seems to have taken the place of her own daughter, and everything she does is intended for Juliet's benefit. The Nurse is a simple soul, and an easy target for Mercutio's ribbing. Her garrulous and often suggestive talk makes us laugh with her rather than at her.

Paris

Paris is a character only lightly sketched but who is nevertheless very real. He is not a villain come to snatch Juliet from Romeo but an honourable suitor whose appearance at this time helps trigger off the tragedy. His words in the tomb show a delicate grief for the girl he hardly knew, and it is his sense of honour, rather than any feelings of jealousy, that causes his outrage at the appearance of Romeo in the tomb.

Romeo

Romeo's character does not develop so quickly or so much as Juliet's, but it has changed quite a lot by the end of the play. In the beginning, he seems to be almost wallowing in self pity; but the chief aspect of his character is his impetuosity. He rushes into love and marriage and his rush back from Mantua, arriving before the Friar, causes the final tragedy. But he changes from a light-hearted man-about-town into a determined adult, who can feel pity for Paris and plan and execute his own death without fear.

Rosaline

Rosaline is important to the plot since it is to see her that Romeo goes to the feast where he meets Juliet, and it is his melancholy love for her that contrasts so dramatically with his happy love for Juliet. Some commentators suggest that she rejects love, as if she is somehow cruel and inhuman; but we have no evidence that she is other than chaste on principle, or perhaps she does not feel affection for Romeo. She is an interesting character, although we never meet her.

Tybalt

Tybalt is a truly one-sided character. The 'Prince of Cats' seems to have no other talent but for arguing, and fighting, at which he has become elegantly expert. Capulet calls him a 'princox' for defying him, but he takes no notice and still seeks out Romeo. It is ironic that it is the death of this violent and unsympathetic character that contributes to the death of the gentle Juliet.

What happens in each act

Act One   The Chorus foretells the tragedy that will take place, and we are then introduced to the feuding families of Montague and Capulet. We hear that Romeo, Montague's son, is very melancholy, and Romeo tells his friend, Benvolio, that it is because of his hopeless love for Rosaline. Because the latter is going to be there, Romeo is persuaded by Benvolio and another friend, Mercutio, to go (uninvited) to a Capulet feast. There he meets Juliet and they fall passionately in love.

Act Two   Romeo cannot keep away from Juliet and goes, straight from the feast, over the wall into her garden. Juliet cannot sleep and appears at her window. They exchange vows of love and decide to be secretly married the next day. The marriage is performed by a Friar the next day as planned, but meanwhile we hear that Tybalt, a belligerent member of the Capulet family who felt insulted by Romeo's presence at the feast, is looking for him in order to kill him.

Act Three   Later the same day, Benvolio, Mercutio and Romeo meet Tybalt who challenges Romeo. Romeo will not fight a man he now feels is a kinsman and Mercutio steps in. Mercutio is killed and Romeo then feels bound to kill Tybalt in revenge. Romeo is punished with exile to Mantua, where he goes after spending his wedding night with Juliet. The plot is now complicated by Capulet's insistence on Juliet's quickly marrying Paris, although she does not wish to.

Act Four   The Friar thinks up a plan to save Juliet. He will give her a drug that will make her appear dead for a while. She will be taken to the Capulet tomb where (later) Romeo will come to her secretly. Unfortunately, the wedding is brought forward by a day; Juliet takes the drug the night before the wedding is due to take place and is mourned as dead.

Act Five   The Friar has sent a message to Romeo in Mantua with the news of his plan by another friar. However, the second friar is held up and Romeo's servant, thinking Juliet is really dead, goes to tell Romeo. Romeo rushes to the tomb and is so devastated by what he finds that he poisons himself. The Friar arrives and Juliet awakes. The Friar tells her that Romeo is dead and asks her to 'come away'. Juliet will not depart. The Friar runs off. Seeing Romeo dead, Juliet stabs herself. The Friar comes back. Shame and sorrow combine to bring Montague and Capulet together. Though Romeo and Juliet are dead, their love has transcended death, and brought peace to the feuding families.

Coursework and preparing for the examination

If you wish to gain a certificate in English literature then there is no substitute for studying the text/s on which you are to be examined. If you cannot be bothered to do that, then neither this guide nor any other will be of use to you.

Here we give advice on studying the text, writing a good essay, producing coursework, and sitting the examination. However, if you meet problems you should ask your teacher for help.

Studying the text

No, not just read – study. You must read your text at least twice. Do not dismiss it if you find a first reading difficult or uninteresting. Approach the text with an open mind and you will often find a second reading more enjoyable. When you become a more experienced reader enjoyment usually follows from a close study of the text, when you begin to appreciate both what the author is saying and the skill with which it is said. Having read the text, you must now study it. We restrict our remarks here to novels and plays, though much of what is said can also be applied to poetry.

1 You will know in full detail all the major incidents in your text, **why**, **where** and **when** they happen, **who** is involved, **what** leads up to them and what follows.

2 You must show that you have an **understanding of the story**, the **characters**, and the **main ideas** which the author is exploring.

3 In a play you must know what happens in each act, and more specifically the organization of the scene structure – how one follows from and builds upon another. Dialogue in both plays and novels is crucial. You must have a detailed knowledge of the major dialogues and soliloquies and the part they play in the development of plot, and the development and drawing of character.

4 When you write about a novel you will not normally be expected to quote or to refer to specific lines but references to incidents and characters must be given, and they must be accurate and specific.

5 In writing about a play you will be expected both to paraphrase dialogue and quote specific lines, always provided, of course, that they are actually contributing something to your essay!

To gain full marks in coursework and/or in an examination you will also be expected to show your own reaction to, and appreciation of, the text studied. The teacher or examiner always welcomes those essays which demonstrate the student's own thoughtful response to the text. Indeed, questions often specify such a requirement, so do participate in those classroom discussions, the debates, class dramatizations of all or selected parts of your text, and the many other activities which enable a class to share and grow in their understanding and feeling for literature.

Making notes

A half-hearted reading of your text, or watching the 'film of the book' will not give you the necessary knowledge to meet the above demands.

As you study the text jot down sequences of events; quotations of note; which events precede and follow the part you are studying; the characters involved; what the part being studied contributes to the plot and your understanding of character and ideas. Write single words, phrases and short sentences which can be quickly reviewed and which will help you to gain a clear picture of the incident being studied. Make your notes neat and orderly, with headings to indicate chapter, scene, page, incident, character, etc, so that you can quickly find the relevant notes or part of the text when revising.

Writing the essay

Good essays are like good books, in miniature; they are thought about, planned, logically structured, paragraphed, have a clearly defined pattern and development of thought, and are presented clearly – and with neat writing! All of this will be to no avail if the tools you use, i.e. words, and the skill with which you put them together to form your sentences and paragraphs are severely limited.

How good is your general and literary vocabulary? Do you understand and can you make appropriate use of such terms as 'soliloquy', 'character', 'plot', 'mood', 'dramatically effective', 'comedy', 'allusion', 'humour', 'imagery', 'irony', 'paradox', 'anti-climax', 'tragedy'? These are all words which examiners have commented on as being misunderstood by students.

Do you understand 'metaphor', 'simile', 'alliteration'? Can you say what their effect is on you, the reader, and how they enable the author to express himself more effectively than by the use of a different literary device? If you cannot, you are employing your time ineffectively by using them.

You are writing an English literature essay and your writing should be literate and appropriate. Slang, colloquialisms and careless use of words are not tolerated in such essays.

Essays for coursework

The exact number of essays you will have to produce and their length will vary; it depends upon the requirements of the examination board whose course you are following, and whether you will be judged solely on coursework or on a mixture of coursework and examination.

As a guide, however your course is structured, you will be required to provide a folder containing at least ten essays, and from that folder five will be selected for moderation purposes. Of those five essays, one will normally have been done in class-time under conditions similar to those of an examination. The essays must cover the complete range of course requirements and be the unaided work of the student. One board specifies that these pieces of continuous writing should be a minimum of 400 words long, and another, a minimum of 500 words long. Ensure that you know what is required for your course, and do not aim for the minimum amount – write a full essay then prune it down if necessary.

Do take care over the presentation of your final folder of coursework. There are many devices on the market which will enable you to bind your work neatly, and in such a way that you can easily insert new pieces. Include a 'Contents' page and a front and back cover to keep your work clean. Ring binders are unsuitable items to hand in for **final** assessment purposes as they are much too bulky.

What sort of coursework essays will you be set? All boards lay down criteria similar to the following for the range of student response to literature that the coursework must cover. Work must demonstrate that the student:

1 shows an understanding not only of surface meaning but also of a deeper awareness of themes and attitudes;

2 recognizes and appreciates ways in which authors use language;

3 recognizes and appreciates ways in which writers achieve their effects, particularly in how the work is structured and in its characterization;

4 can write imaginatively in exploring and developing ideas so as to communicate a sensitive and informed personal response to what is read.

Much of what is said in the section **Writing essays in an examination** on p 76 is relevant here, but for coursework essays you have the advantage of plenty of time to prepare your work – so take advantage of it.

There is no substitute for arguing, discussing and talking about a question on a particular text or theme. Your teacher should give you plenty of opportunity for this in the classroom. Listening to what others say about a subject often opens up for you new ways to look at and respond to it. The same can be said for reading about a topic. Be careful not to copy down slavishly what others say and write. Jot down notes then go away and think about what you have heard, read and written. Make more notes of your own and then start to clarify your own thoughts, feelings and emotions on the subject about which you are writing. Most students make the mistake of doing their coursework essays in a rush - you have time so use it.

Take a great deal of care in planning your work. From all your notes, write a rough draft and then start the task of really perfecting it.

1 Look at your arrangement of paragraphs, is there a logical development of thought or argument? Do the paragraphs need rearranging in order? Does the first or last sentence of any paragraph need redrafting in order to provide a sensible link with the preceding or next paragraph?

2 Look at the pattern of sentences within each paragraph. Are your thoughts and ideas clearly developed and expressed? Have you used any quotations, paraphrases,

or references to incidents to support your opinions and ideas? Are those references relevant and apt, or just 'padding'?

3 Look at the words and phrases you have used. Do not repeat words in close proximity one to another. Are the words you have used to comment on the text being studied the most appropriate and effective, or just the first ones you thought of?

4 Check your spelling and punctuation.

5 Now write a final draft, the quality of which should reflect the above considerations.

Writing essays in an examination

Read the question. Identify the key words and phrases. Write them down, and as they are dealt with in your essay plan, tick them off.

Plan your essay. Spend about five minutes jotting down ideas; organize your thoughts and ideas into a logical and developing order – a structure is essential to the production of a good essay. Remember, brief, essential notes only!

Write your essay

How long should it be? There is no magic length. What you must do is answer the question set, fully and sensitively in the time allowed. You will probably have about forty minutes to answer an essay question, and within that time you should produce an essay between roughly 350 and 500 words in length. Very short answers will not do justice to the question, very long answers will probably contain much irrelevant information and waste time that should be spent on the next answer.

How much quotation? Use only that which is apt and contributes to the clarity and quality of your answer. No examiner will be impressed by 'padding'.

What will the examiners be looking for in an essay?

1 An answer to the question set, and not a prepared answer to another, albeit slightly similar question done in class.

2 A well-planned, logically structured and paragraphed essay with a beginning, middle and end.

3 Accurate references to plot, character, theme, as required by the question.

4 Appropriate, brief, and if needed, frequent quotation and references to support and demonstrate the comments that you are making in your essay.

5 Evidence that reading the text has prompted in you a personal response to it, as well as some judgment and appreciation of its literary merit.

How do you prepare to do this?

1 During your course you should write between three to five essays on each text.

2 Make good use of class discussion etc, as mentioned in a previous paragraph on page 75.

3 Try to see a live performance of a play. It may help to see a film of a play or book, though be aware that directors sometimes leave out episodes, change their order, or worse, add episodes that are not in the original – so be very careful. In the end, there is no substitute for **reading and studying** the text!

Try the following exercises without referring to any notes or text.

1 Pick a character from your text.

2 Make a list of his/her qualities – both positive and negative ones, or aspects that you cannot quite define. Jot down single words to describe each quality. If you do not know the word you want, use a thesaurus, but use it in conjunction with a dictionary and make sure you are fully aware of the meaning of each word you use.

3 Write a short sentence which identifies one or more places in the text where you think each quality is demonstrated.

4 Jot down any brief quotation, paraphrase of conversation or outline of an incident which shows that quality.

5 Organize the list. Identify groupings which contrast the positive and negative aspects of character.

6 Write a description of that character which makes full use of the material you have just prepared.

7 What do you think of the character you have just described? How has he/she reacted to and coped with the pressures of the other characters, incidents, and the setting of the story? Has he/she changed in any way? In no more than 100 words, including 'evidence' taken from the text, write a balanced assessment of the character, and draw some conclusions.

You should be able to do the above without notes, and without the text, unless you are to take an examination which allows the use of plain texts. In plain text examinations you are allowed to take in a copy of your text. It must be without notes, either your own or the publisher's. The intention is to enable you to consult a text in the examination so as to confirm memory of detail, thus enabling a candidate to quote and refer more accurately in order to illustrate his/her views that more effectively. Examiners will expect a high standard of accurate reference, quotation and comment in a plain text examination.

Sitting the examination

You will have typically between two and five essays to write and you will have roughly 40 minutes, on average, to write each essay.

On each book you have studied, you should have a choice of doing at least one out of two or three essay titles set.

1 **Before sitting the exam**, make sure you are completely clear in your mind that you know exactly how many questions you must answer, which sections of the paper you must tackle, and how many questions you may, or must, attempt on any one book or in any one section of the paper. If you are not sure, ask your teacher.

2 **Always read the instructions** given at the top of your examination paper. They are there to help you. Take your time, and try to relax – panicking is not going to help.

3 **Be very clear about timing, and organizing your time**
(a) Know how long the examination is.
(b) Know how many questions you must do.
(c) Divide (b) into (a) to work out how long you may spend on each question. (Bear in mind that some questions may attract more marks, and should therefore take proportionately more time.)
(d) Keep an eye on the time, and do not spend more than you have allowed for any one question.
(e) If you have spare time at the end you can come back to a question and do more work on it.
(f) Do not be afraid to jot down notes as an aid to memory, but do cross them out carefully after use – a single line will do!

4 **Do not rush the decision** as to which question you are going to answer on a particular text.
(a) Study each question carefully.
(b) Be absolutely sure what each one is asking for.
(c) Make your decision as to which you will answer.

5 **Having decided which question** you will attempt:
(a) jot down the key points of the actual question – use single words or short phrases.
(b) think about how you are going to arrange your answer. Five minutes here, with some notes jotted down will pay dividends later.
(c) write your essay, and keep an eye on the time!

6 **Adopt the same approach** for all questions. Do write answers for the maximum number of questions you are told to attempt. One left out will lose its proportion of the total marks. Remember also, you will never be awarded extra marks, over and above those already allocated, if you write an extra long essay on a particular question.

7 **Do not waste time** on the following:
(a) an extra question – you will get no marks for it.
(b) worrying about how much anyone else is writing, they can't help you!
(c) relaxing at the end with time to spare – you do not have any. Work up to the very moment the invigilator tells you to stop writing. Check and recheck your work, including spelling and punctuation. Every single mark you gain helps, and that last mark might tip the balance between success and failure – the line has to be drawn somewhere.

8 **Help the examiner**
(a) Do not use red or green pen or pencil on your paper. Examiners usually annotate your script in red and green, and if you use the same colours it will cause unnecessary confusion.
(b) Leave some space between each answer or section of an answer. This could also help you if you remember something you wish to add to your answer when you are checking it.
(c) Number your answers as instructed. If it is question 3 you are doing, do not label it 'C'.
(d) Write neatly. It will help you to communicate effectively with the examiner who is trying to read your script.

Glossary of literary terms

Mere knowledge of the words in this list or other specialist words used when studying literature is not sufficient. You must know when to use a particular term, and be able to describe what it contributes to that part of the work which is being discussed.

For example, merely to label something as being a metaphor does not help an examiner or teacher to assess your response to the work being studied. You must go on to analyse what the literary device contributes to the work. Why did the author use a metaphor at all? Why not some other literary device? What extra sense of feeling or meaning does the metaphor convey to the reader? How effective is it in supporting the author's intention? What was the author's intention, as far as you can judge, in using that metaphor?

Whenever you use a particular literary term you must do so with a purpose and that purpose usually involves an explanation and expansion upon its use. Occasionally you will simply use a literary term 'in passing', as, for example, when you refer to the 'narrator' of a story as opposed to the 'author' – they are not always the same! So please be sure that you understand both the meaning and purpose of each literary term you employ.

This list includes only those words which we feel will assist in helping you to understand the major concepts in play and novel construction. It makes no attempt to be comprehensive. These are the concepts which examiners frequently comment upon as being inadequately grasped by many students. Your teacher will no doubt expand upon this list and introduce you to other literary devices and words within the context of the particular work/s you are studying – the most useful place to experience and explore them and their uses.

Plot This is the plan or story of a play or novel. Just as a body has a skeleton to hold it together, so the plot forms the 'bare bones' of the work of literature in play or novel form. It is however, much more than this. It is arranged in time, so one of the things which encourages us to continue reading is to see what happens next. It deals with causality, that is how one event or incident causes another. It has a sequence, so that in general, we move from the beginning through to the end.

Structure The arrangement and interrelationship of parts in a play or novel are obviously bound up with the plot. An examination of how the author has structured his work will lead us to consider the function of, say, the 43 letters which are such an important part of *Pride and Prejudice*. We would consider the arrangement of the time-sequence in *Wuthering Heights* with its 'flashbacks' and their association with the different narrators of the story. In a play we would look at the scene divisions and how different events are placed in a relationship so as to produce a particular effect; where soliloquies occur so as to inform the audience of a character's innermost emotions and feelings. Do be aware that great works of fiction are not just simply thrown together by their authors. We study a work in detail, admiring its parts and the intricacies of its structure. The reason for a work's greatness has to do with the genius of its author and the care of its construction. Ultimately, though, we do well to remember that it is the work as a whole that we have to judge, not just the parts which make up that whole.

Narrator   A narrator tells or relates a story. In *Wuthering Heights* various characters take on the task of narrating the events of the story: Cathy, Heathcliff, etc, as well as being, at other times, central characters taking their part in the story. Sometimes the author will be there, as it were, in person, relating and explaining events. The method adopted in telling the story relates very closely to style and structure.

Style   The manner in which something is expressed or performed, considered as separate from its intrinsic content or meaning. It might well be that a lyrical, almost poetical style will be used, for example concentrating on the beauties and contrasts of the natural world as a foil to the narration of the story and creating emotions in the reader which serve to heighten reactions to the events being played out on the page. It might be that the author uses a terse, almost staccato approach to the conveyance of his story. There is no simple route to grasping the variations of style which are to be found between different authors or indeed within one novel. The surest way to appreciate this difference is to read widely and thoughtfully and to analyse and appreciate the various strategies which an author uses to command our attention.

Character   A person represented in a play or story. However, the word also refers to the combination of traits and qualities distinguishing the individual nature of a person or thing. Thus, a characteristic is one such distinguishing quality: in *Pride and Prejudice*, the pride and prejudices of various characters are central to the novel, and these characteristics which are associated with Mr Darcy, Elizabeth, and Lady Catherine in that novel, enable us to begin assessing how a character is reacting to the surrounding events and people. Equally, the lack of a particular trait or characteristic can also tell us much about a character.

Character development   In *Pride and Prejudice*, the extent to which Darcy's pride, or Elizabeth's prejudice is altered, the recognition by those characters of such change, and the events of the novel which bring about the changes are central to any exploration of how a character develops, for better or worse.

Irony   This is normally taken to be the humorous or mildly sarcastic use of words to imply the opposite of what they say. It also refers to situations and events and thus you will come across references such as prophetic, tragic, and dramatic irony.

Dramatic irony   This occurs when the implications of a situation or speech are understood by the audience but not by all or some of the characters in the play or novel. We also class as ironic words spoken innocently but which a later event proves either to have been mistaken or to have prophesied that event. When we read in the play *Macbeth*:

> *Macbeth*
> Tonight we hold a solemn supper, sir,
> And I'll request your presence.

> *Banquo*
> Let your highness
> Command upon me, to the which my duties
> Are with a most indissoluble tie
> Forever knit.

we, as the audience, will shortly have revealed to us the irony of Macbeth's words. He does not expect Banquo to attend the supper as he plans to have Banquo murdered before the supper occurs. However, what Macbeth does not know is the prophetic irony of Banquo's response. His 'duties. . . a most indissoluble tie' will be fulfilled by his appearance at the supper as a ghost – something Macbeth certainly did not forsee or welcome, and which Banquo most certainly did not have in mind!

Tragedy   This is usually applied to a play in which the main character, usually a person of importance and outstanding personal qualities, falls to disaster through the combination of personal failing and circumstances with which he cannot deal. Such tragic happenings may also be central to a novel. In *The Mayor of Casterbridge*, flaws in Henchard's character are partly responsible for his downfall and eventual death.

In Shakespeare's plays, *Macbeth* and *Othello*, the tragic heroes from which the two plays take their names, are both highly respected and honoured men who have proven their outstanding personal qualities. Macbeth, driven on by his ambition and that of his very determined wife, kills his king. It leads to civil war in his country, to his own eventual downfall and death, and to his wife's suicide. Othello, driven to an insane jealousy by the cunning of his lieutenant, Iago, murders his own innocent wife and commits suicide.

Satire   Where topical issues, folly or evil are held up to scorn by means of ridicule and irony – the satire may be subtle or openly abusive.

In *Animal Farm*, George Orwell used the rebellion of the animals against their oppressive owner to satirize the excesses of the Russian revolution at the beginning of the 20th century. It would be a mistake, however, to see the satire as applicable only to that event. There is a much wider application of that satire to political and social happenings both before and since the Russian revolution and in all parts of the world.

Images   An image is a mental representation or picture. One that constantly recurs in *Macbeth* is clothing, sometimes through double meanings of words: 'he seems rapt withal', 'Why do you dress me in borrowed robes?', 'look how our partner's rapt', 'Like our strange garments, cleave not to their mould', 'Whiles I stood rapt in the wonder of it', 'which would be worn now in their newest gloss', 'Was the hope drunk Wherein you dressed yourself?', 'Lest our old robes sit easier than our new.', 'like a giant's robe upon a dwarfish thief'. All these images serve to highlight and comment upon aspects of Macbeth's behaviour and character. In Act 5, Macbeth the loyal soldier who was so honoured by his king at the start of the play, struggles to regain some small shred of his self-respect. Three times he calls to Seyton for his armour, and finally moves toward his destiny with the words 'Blow wind, come wrack, At least we'll die with harness on our back' – his own armour, not the borrowed robes of a king he murdered.

Do remember that knowing a list of images is not sufficient. You must be able to interpret them and comment upon the contribution they make to the story being told.

Theme   A unifying idea, image or motif, repeated or developed throughout a work.

In *Pride and Prejudice*, a major theme is marriage. During the course of the novel we are shown various views of and attitudes towards marriage. We actually witness the relationships of four different couples through their courtship, engagement and eventual marriage. Through those events and the examples presented to us in the novel of other already married couples, the author engages in a thorough exploration of the theme.

This list is necessarily short. There are whole books devoted to the explanation of literary terms. Some concepts, like style, need to be experienced and discussed in a group setting with plenty of examples in front of you. Others, such as dramatic irony, need keen observation from the student and a close knowledge of the text to appreciate their significance and existence. All such specialist terms are well worth knowing. But they should be used only if they enable you to more effectively express your knowledge and appreciation of the work being studied.